MHCC WITHDRAWN

D0450430

INSIGHT GUIDES

IRELAND
StepbyStep

APA PUBLICATIONS **L**

Part of the Langenscheidt Publishing Group

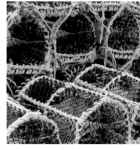
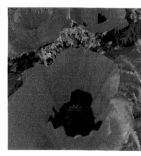

CONTENTS

Above: rural residents; café chalkboard; Georgian door-knocker in Dublin; live traditional music abounds in Ireland; wool produced at the Sheep and Wool Centre in Lenane.

ABOUT THIS BOOK

This *Step by Step Guide* has been produced by the editors of Insight Guides, whose books have set the standard for visual travel guides since 1970. With top-quality photography and authoritative recommendations, this guidebook brings you the very best of Ireland in a series of 16 tailor-made tours.

WALKS AND TOURS

The tours in the book provide something to suit all budgets, tastes and trip lengths. They begin with two walks exploring the Irish capital, Dublin, followed by a series of drives and walks that travel clockwise around the country, ending with a detour to Belfast, capital of Northern Ireland. The tours embrace a range of interests, so whether you are an art fan, a gourmet, a lover of flora or have kids to entertain, you will find an option to suit.

We recommend reading the whole of a tour before setting out. This will help you to familiarise yourself with the route and enable you to plan where to stop for refreshments – options for this are shown in the 'Food and Drink' boxes, recognisable by the knife-and-fork sign, on most pages.

For our pick of the walks by theme, consult Recommended Tours For… *(see pp.6–7).*

OVERVIEW

The tours are set in context by this introductory section, giving an overview of the island to set the scene, plus background information on food and drink, shopping, entertainment and outdoor activities. A succinct history timeline highlights the key events that have shaped Ireland over the centuries.

DIRECTORY

Also supporting the tours is a Directory chapter, comprising a user-friendly, clearly organised A–Z of practical information, our pick of where to stay while you are in Ireland and select restaurant listings; these eateries complement the more low-key cafés and restaurants that feature within the tours and are intended to offer a wider choice for evening dining. Also included here are some nightlife listings.

The Authors

The second edition of this book has been thoroughly updated by original writer **Alannah Hopkin**, who has lived in Kinsale since 1982, working as a writer and frequently contributing to Insight's Irish titles. She still enjoys exploring her adopted home and showing friends around. Once they have got over the amazing scenery and the slower pace of life, what impresses her visitors most is the locals' genuine friendliness.

The walks in Dublin and Belfast, and the tours of counties Wicklow, Sligo and Donegal, were originally written by **Tara Stubbs**, who has a PhD in Irish literature and culture from Oxford University.

Margin Tips
Shopping tips, historical facts, handy hints and information on activities help visitors to make the most of their time in Ireland.

Feature Boxes
Notable topics are highlighted in these special boxes.

Key Facts Box
This box gives details of the distance covered on the tour, plus an estimate of how long it should take. It also states where the route starts and finishes, and gives key travel information such as which days are best to do the route or handy transport tips.

Route Map
Detailed cartography shows the tour clearly plotted with numbered dots. For more detailed mapping, see the pull-out map slotted inside the back cover.

Footers
Look here for the tour name, a map reference and the main attraction on the double-page.

Food and Drink
Recommendations of where to stop for refreshment are given in these boxes. The numbers prior to each restaurant/café name link to references in the main text. Restaurants in the Food and Drink boxes are plotted on the maps.

The € (Irish Republic) and £ (Northern Ireland) signs at the end of each entry reflect the approximate cost of a two-course dinner for one, excluding drinks. These should be seen as a guide only. Price ranges, also quoted on the inside back flap for easy reference, are:

€€€€	over 40 euros	££££	over £40
€€€	30–40 euros	£££	£25–40
€€	20–30 euros	££	£15–25
€	under 20 euros	£	under £15

CELTIC ROMANCE

Glimpse the round tower through the Celtic mist at Glendalough (tour 3), enjoy a kingly view from the Rock of Cashel (tour 5), climb mystical Knocknarea (tour 15) or venture over the sea to Skellig Michael (tour 8).

RECOMMENDED TOURS FOR...

CHILDREN

Shout out loud on a Viking Splash Tour in Dublin (walk 1), visit a 19th-century 'coffin ship' in New Ross (tour 4), get up close to the animals at Fota Wildlife Park (tour 6) or play games on endless stretches of sand in County Donegal (tour 15).

GARDENERS

Powerscourt Gardens (tour 3) are considered among the finest in Europe. Bantry House (tour 7) has terraced gardens overlooking the bay, and do not miss the Palm House in Belfast's Botanic Gardens (walk 16).

LITERARY TYPES

The *Book of Kells* is at Trinity College (walk 1), alma mater of many Irish writers, but not W.B. Yeats, who preferred Sligo (tour 15). The Dublin Writers' Museum (walk 2) will explain why.

NEW IRISH CUISINE

The restaurants of St Stephen's Green and Merrion Row in Dublin (walk 2), The Tannery in Waterford (tour 5 and p.117) and The Park Hotel in Kenmare (tour 8) are the stars of a dazzling new generation. Relaxed Belfast has a host of exciting eating options (walk 16).

WALKERS

Walk across heathery hills on the Dingle Way (tour 9), explore the eerie limestone plateau of the Burren (tour 11), marvel at Connemara's huge skies (tour 13) or follow the Wicklow Way (tour 3).

NATURAL WONDERS

The 40,000 hexagonal basalt columns of the Giant's Causeway (tour 16) in Northern Ireland are beyond strange. The Cliffs of Moher (tour 11) will take your breath away, as will the view of Clew Bay from Croaghpatrick (tour 14). Gaze in awe at the tumultuous waves below Slieve League in County Donegal (tour 15).

PICTUREBOOK VILLAGES

Choose from the pretty thatched cottages of Adare (tour 10), Kinvara's stone quays and views of Galway Bay (tour 11), or Lismore (tour 5) with its fairytale castle above the wooded Blackwater Valley.

SHOPPERS

Buy your beloved a Claddagh ring in Galway (walk 12), treat yourself to some Jerpoint Glass in Kilkenny (tour 4) or some handwoven linens in Avoca (tour 3), invest in Waterford Crystal (tour 5), or simply go mad on the high street in Dublin and Belfast (walks 1, 2 and 16).

MODERN & CONTEMPORARY ART

The National Gallery's Millennium Wing (walk 2) will introduce you to contemporary Irish art. See more Jack B. Yeats in the galleries of Sligo (tour 15). Dublin's City Gallery The Hugh Lane (tour 2), and Cork's Crawford Gallery (tour 6) are also highlights not to be missed.

OVERVIEW

An overview of Ireland's geography, character and culture, plus illuminating background information on food and drink, shopping, entertainment, outdoor activities and history.

INTRODUCTION

Ireland is Europe's most westerly outpost, swathed with vast areas of unspoilt wilderness, dotted with romantic ruins and yet also boasting one of Europe's liveliest capital cities, Dublin, where the population is becoming more racially diverse, adding new strands to its thriving arts scene.

Above: English and Irish signposts in County Clare; hand-cut turf by the roadside in Donegal.

Ireland is a land of contrasts and contradictions. It is famous for capitalising on its membership of the European Union, yet is also a place apart as the westernmost land mass in Europe, where serried ranges of scantly inhabited hills lead to a rugged Atlantic coast, and the legacy of its Celtic and Gaelic past persists. Throughout your travels, you will encounter the contrast of the old and traditional alongside the new. Many heritage sites have bold modern architectural additions, and even the 'jarveys' driving the horse-drawn sidecars in Killarney take their bookings by mobile phone.

GEOGRAPHY AND LAYOUT

The island of Ireland contains two separate countries: the Republic of Ireland and Northern Ireland. The latter, in the northeastern corner of the island, is part of the UK. In its entirety, the island covers 84,288 sq km (32,544 sq miles), measuring 485km (302 miles) at its longest point and 304km (189 miles) at its widest, while its coastline extends for around 5,630km (3,500 miles). Low ranges of mountains surround a central lowland area of limestone, much of which is covered in peat bogs.

Getting Around

Public transport is a weak point. While the railways link the peripheral towns to Dublin, the lines do not interconnect to any useful extent. Neither is bus travel satisfactory for touring. If you are intending to visit rural Ireland, the only comfortable option is by car.

The tours in this guide begin with two walks exploring the historic and modern faces of the Irish capital Dublin, before a series of drives and walks that travel clockwise around the

country, down the east coast, along the south and up the west, ending in Northern Ireland. Verdant Wicklow is an easy day trip from Dublin; then the tours visit Kilkenny, Waterford and the iconic Rock of Cashel, all of which are only a short distance from the main Dublin–Cork road. After a walk through Cork's medieval streets and Victorian harbour, the tours continue along the scenic coast of west Cork and Kerry to the Dingle Peninsula, before exploring 'castle country' around the Shannon Estuary, visiting Adare, Limerick and Bunratty. The tours then proceed northwards up the more exposed west coast from the strange limestone plateau known as the Burren in County Clare to vibrant Galway city. A day-long drive through ruggedly beautiful Connemara leads towards charming Westport town and scenic County Mayo. Further north, Sligo town and the surrounding countryside were made famous in the poems of W.B. Yeats, while County Donegal has some lovely beaches. From here, we cross the border to visit Northern Ireland's fast-changing capital, Belfast, with a detour to the Giant's Causeway.

HISTORY & ARCHITECTURE

The early settlers left their marks all over the land, from megalithic tombs in the Boyne Valley to the mysterious stone circles of west Cork and Kerry. Later,

the flourishing of Irish monasticism in the 6th to 9th centuries bequeathed the beautiful ruins at Glendalough and Cashel. The first hostile invaders were the Vikings in the 9th century, but they, like the Anglo-Normans who followed, intermarried and were absorbed into Irish society. The rich lived in tower houses or castles, like Blarney and Bunratty, fortified against tribal warfare. They also introduced Continental orders like the Cistercians, and endowed monasteries such as Jerpoint Abbey in County Kilkenny.

Henry VIII's decision in 1541 to impose English rule – and what would become the Protestant religion – on Ireland, which shared its Catholic loyalties with England's enemies, France and Spain, had long-running repercussions. Walled towns like Cork, Galway, Kilkenny and Waterford were used for refuge by English settlers, sent to Ireland to swell the numbers loyal to the king.

The coming of more peaceful times in the 18th and 19th century saw the construction of Georgian Dublin, as well as the elaborate 'big houses' (as the Irish call stately homes) scattered throughout the countryside, many with ambitious gardens.

From Famine to Feast

Ireland was devastated by the Great Famine of 1845–9, when about 1 million people died and another million emigrated, leaving vast tracts of land

Above from far left: the 'savage beauty' of Connemara; Tigh Neachtain, a traditional pub and arts hub in Galway; winding roads in Donegal.

Tribal Chief
In old Gaelic society people owed allegiance to the tribal chief or *taoiseach* (pronounced 'tee-shock'). It is often suggested that Irish politics has developed along similar lines. It is remarkable for its dynasties, with seats being handed down from father to son or daughter. One exception was Bertie Ahern, *taoiseach* (prime minister) from 1997–2008; his daughter Cecilia is a best-selling author, while daughter Georgina married Nicky Byrne of boy band Westlife.

Above from left:
the first monastic settlement at Glendalough was established in 498AD; Celtic crosses; cherub at the Powerscourt Estate; enjoying a pint.

uninhabited. There followed a century of political unrest and economic depression, and only in the past 30 years has Ireland recovered, changing from a backward-looking society to one of the most cosmopolitan and culturally successful (from Seamus Heaney to U2 to *Riverdance*) in Europe. The development of its tourist industry, aided by the availability of cheap flights, saw 5.8 million visitors in 2010, generating €3.8 billion in revenue.

CLIMATE

Ireland has a mild maritime climate with temperate summers. July is the warmest month with temperatures averaging 14–15°C (57–9°F), and February is the coldest with averages of 4–5°C (39–41°F).

Rainfall increases as you travel west. Between December and March, cold and rainy weather can persist everywhere. In winter the days are short, with the sun setting at around 4.30pm by the solstice (21 December). In contrast, summer evenings are long, with daylight until 10pm or later. July and August are the best months for hot sunny weather, but this is never predictable. These months are also the high season for Irish family holidays, and prices and pressure on facilities rise accordingly. The best times to visit are late spring and early autumn; May to June, and September and October.

POPULATION

The population of the Republic of Ireland is approximately 4.5 million, while Northern Ireland's population is just under 1.75 million. Over 40 percent of the population of the Republic live within 100km (62 miles) of Dublin.

Ireland's population declined during the 20th century, chiefly due to emigration, and only stabilised in the late-1980s, growing steadily throughout the 1990s. The expansion of the EU in 2004 led to a new wave of immigrants, chiefly from Eastern Europe, but also from Africa, where Irish missionaries have long been active in education. The impact of the economic downturn following the financial crisis of 2008 has led to a rise in emigration once more, with many Eastern European workers returning home, and Irish people moving overseas to find work.

POLITICS & ECONOMICS

The Republic's two main parties have their origins in Ireland's Civil War (1922–3): Fianna Fáil (Warriors of Ireland) traditionally draws its support from small farmers, the urban working class and entrepreneurs, while Fine Gael (Tribes of Ireland) is supported by larger-scale farmers and the professional classes. Left and right wing mean very little in Irish politics. Because of proportional representation, most governments are coalitions.

Where is Everyone?
About 1.5 million of the Republic's 4.5 million population live in Dublin, which is much like any other city – fast-paced and stressful, with gridlocked traffic. Outside Dublin, the average density is 57 people per sq km (148 per square mile). In remote regions like west Cork and Kerry, the average falls to around 27 people per sq km. To get a feel for Ireland, it really is necessary to travel beyond Dublin.

The Troubles

From 1969, the international view of Irish politics was dominated for 30 years by outbreaks of violence, mainly in localised areas of Northern Ireland, known as 'The Troubles'. This unhappy era began when a civil rights demonstration was attacked by loyalists (those loyal to the British Crown). The IRA intensified its 'armed struggle' in Northern Ireland, seeking the unification of the island under Irish administration. Between 1969 and 2001, 3,526 people were killed in the struggle, about two thirds of them civilians. Eventually a compromise was reached, in which the Republic amended its constitution to abandon its claims of sovereignty over Northern Ireland and the IRA agreed to lay down its arms. Elected Protestant and Republican leaders agreed to enter a power-sharing assembly at Stormont in Belfast, and work together for the good of Northern Ireland.

Economics

The Republic is still reeling from the world economic downturn, and reeling too from revelations of dubious practices among bankers and property developers, the bill for which is being passed to the taxpayer. The worldwide recession coupled with the strong euro has hit the tourism sector, but the reaction has been up-beat: prices have been slashed and special offers abound. Restaurants and hotels that were not up to the grade are disappearing off the scene, and those that remain are trying harder than ever to please, making this a very good time to visit Ireland.

A WARM WELCOME

While nobody goes to Ireland for the weather, and the prices may not be cheap, the country has managed to combine modern comforts and traditional hospitality in an attractive way. The people have an outstanding capacity for enjoyment, and have retained a natural courtesy and friendliness that has disappeared elsewhere. When asked what they like best about Ireland, for most visitors the answer is 'the Irish people'.

Sleepy Sundays

Although local shops and supermarkets open on Sundays, bars and most restaurants remain closed until around 12.30pm. If you are travelling and looking for a stopping place, the best option is often a hotel. Dublin and other cities are dead as a doornail on Sunday mornings, with many attractions closed until 2pm or indeed all day long.

Irish Literature

The Irish love telling stories, and listening to them too. Before the written word, travelling storytellers (seanchai) entertained beside the fire. The tradition of impromptu verbal wit lives on with Irish comedians and broadcasters. English spoken and written in Ireland differs from English elsewhere, with echoes of Irish-language words and constructions persisting. Jonathan Swift (1667–1745), satirist and author of *Gulliver's Travels*, and dramatist Oscar Wilde (1854–1900) are among the Irish writers whose works continue to be enjoyed worldwide. For a small country, Ireland has an impressive roster of winners of the Nobel Prize for Literature: George Bernard Shaw (1856–1950), W.B. Yeats (1865–1939), Samuel Beckett (1906–89) and Seamus Heaney (1939–). Literary festivals are convivial, informal events, where authors and the reading public mingle freely. The biggest one of all is Bloomsday (16 June), a four-day event that commemorates James Joyce's *Ulysses* (1922) in its Dublin setting (see www.visitdublin.com).

FOOD & DRINK

Ireland has an abundance of farm-fresh produce and sea-fresh fish, but only recently has a distinctive style of Irish cooking emerged. A new generation of chefs is creating an exciting new dining experience at all price levels.

Traditionally, Irish food was plain but hearty. Bread and potatoes accompanied the main meal; a meat stew if you were lucky, or fish on Fridays. Vegetables were boiled to a pulp and salads were a rare summer treat. Garlic, avocados and aubergines were unheard of in most homes. However, in one generation Irish cooking has changed beyond all recognition. There is a new awareness of the amazing raw materials available to chefs in the form of grass-fed beef and lamb, fresh seafood from the Atlantic, abundant dairy produce and home-grown vegetables and salads. Even the humble Irish soda bread, made without yeast or other additives, and once considered inferior to shop-bought white bread, has come to be valued for its health-giving wholesomeness. Try a classic treat of six raw oysters, soda bread and half a pint of black stout to understand its appeal.

LOCAL CUISINE

Ireland's high-quality produce is imaginatively prepared by today's chefs to emphasise its freshness, flavour and texture. Ireland's chefs work closely with artisan food producers, who use traditional methods to smoke fish and make charcuterie and farmhouse cheeses. Many restaurants grow their own salads and herbs, or have an arrangement with a local grower. When people eat out, they have come to expect a high standard of cuisine, whether at an expensive restaurant or at the local café.

Irish chefs are trained in the classic tradition, and most go abroad for a few years and bring back culinary influences from their travels – generally Mediterranean, but sometimes eastern – adapting them to the Irish market. This eclectic approach is also followed by Ireland's private cookery schools, the best known being Ballymaloe Cookery School near the famous country house hotel. Darina Allen, its director, has been preaching the doctrine of using fresh local produce, treated with simplicity and respect, since 1983, and has trained many of today's Irish chefs. In Belfast, which has a fast-growing restaurant scene, young chefs vie for the privilege of working in the kitchen of Paul and Jeanne Rankin, pioneers of new Irish cuisine, at their flagship Cayenne restaurant.

Farmers' Markets

Farmers' markets, where producers sell directly to the public, are a great addition to the Irish food scene. They are ideal for picnic food, offering local farmhouse cheeses, charcuterie and patés. Traditional breads and baking are also a strong point, as are jams, chutneys and sauces, and fresh organic salads, fruit and vegetables. Check out www.bordbia.ie

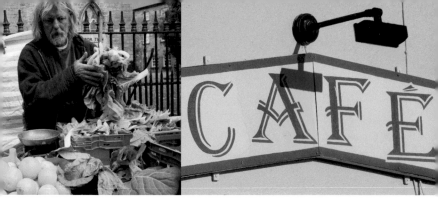

Traditonal Favourites

The fondness for the potato continues to be a national characteristic. The humble 'spud' will often be served in three different ways – mashed, chipped and dauphinoise, for example. Many Irish people like to order steak when they eat out, and it will be found on even the fanciest of menus.

Many people also eat their main meal – known as dinner – at midday. Pubs advertising 'carvery lunches' offer two or three roast meats carved to order at a self-service counter, with a selection of traditional vegetables, and, of course, spuds. Another favourite is fish and chips, traditionally eaten as a take-away in the street, but now served even in the most upmarket restaurants, like Kinsale's Fishy Fishy. Bread (served with butter on the side) has become a star turn in Irish restaurants, with most places baking their own or buying it in from a specialist bakery.

Farm to Fork

All meat in Ireland is now traceable back to the farm, and the flavour of locally reared and butchered meat comes as a pleasant surprise. The Irish Food Board runs a programme, Féile Bia, encouraging restaurants to source as much as possible of their food locally and pass on the information about its provenance to their customers. 'Bia' is the Irish word for food, and 'féile' means both festival and celebration. These words on the menu mean that the restaurant is committed to serving carefully sourced fresh local produce. This will often be game in the autumn and winter, such as venison, pheasant, duck and woodcock.

Above from far left: oysters fresh from the Atlantic; spuds are still a favourite; fresh produce at a farmers' market; café in Kinvara.

Left: stout and soda bread.

WHERE TO EAT

Fine Dining

Some 50 years ago, there were hardly any restaurants in Ireland apart from hotel dining rooms, especially in provincial towns. Even today, some of the best restaurants are still to be found in hotels, such as the Park Hotel Kenmare on the Ring of Kerry. Even in Dublin, hotel restaurants are chic, none more so than The Tea Room at the U2-owned Clarence Hotel. Many hotels have two or more restaurants, one for fine dining and another informal. They also have the advantage of being open daily, whereas many Irish restaurants close after Sunday lunch and do not serve dinner on Sunday or Monday. Booking is advisable at most restaurants, but even the best, like Dublin's top places, Restaurant Patrick Guilbaud, Chapter One, Thorntons and L'Ecrivain, are relatively informal, specifying only 'smart casual' at dinner. If you want to treat yourself, remember that lunch is generally less expensive than dinner. Restaurants often have special-value 'early bird' menus for diners who arrive before 7 or 7.30pm.

Bistros, Wine Bars & Brasseries

The Irish have an idiosyncratic way with these terms, all of which can be interpreted as an 'informal, fun place without tablecloths'. A high rate of VAT and high overheads make it very difficult to run a stylish and good-value establishment, but people do try, like the Chatham Brasserie in Dublin, The Chart House in Dingle town or the Silver Apple in Sligo. An increasingly popular way of keeping prices down is to offer a tapas menu, where dishes can be shared, such as the Market Bar in Dublin. Northern Ireland is better value, thanks to the weak pound; in Belfast seek out the brasseries along Botanic Avenue for good-quality food at student-friendly prices.

Pubs

Since the introduction of the smoking ban and drink-driving laws, pubs have had to diversify. Nearly everywhere now serves tea and coffee, and espresso machines are commonplace in city pubs. More are serving food, often

Below: the Irish scone tends to be huge, and is served warm with cream as well as with butter and strawberry jam. They are just as popular with morning coffee as with afternoon tea.

with an all-day menu that may feature soups, sandwiches, salads and a couple of hot dishes, or at a self-service 'carvery' *(see p.15)*. The best pub food is found in places that offer daily specials at lunchtime and in the early evening, like The Locke Bar in Limerick city. Most pubs stop serving food at around 9pm, to make more room for drinkers. Some pubs, like Vaughan's Anchor Inn in Liscannor, have effectively turned into restaurants that also serve drinks, with waiter service at all tables. Others, like Moran's Oyster Cottage in Kilcolgan, have a separate restaurant area with a full menu. Children are welcome in most food-serving pubs in the daytime, and some even have play areas and children's menus.

Daytime Cafés

Since the Irish acquired a taste for real coffee, cafés have bucked up no end. They usually offer some form of home-baking, often the ubiquitous scone or a warm slice of quiche, as well as sandwiches, salads and home-made soups, and perhaps a pasta option.

DRINKS

Irish pubs are expensive. A pint of beer in Dublin will set you back about €5 (compared to about €3.80 in a rural pub), and a soft drink can cost €4. Wine by the glass goes from about €4.50 in a country pub to €8 or more in a fancy Dublin hotel. Try to be philosophical: you are not just paying for the drink, you are paying for the experience of being in a real Irish pub. With any luck, you will get some free live music (most likely after 10pm), or some witty conversation.

Irish Stout

Irish pubs sell the usual range of beer and lager, bottled and on tap, in measures of a pint or half pint, but the one that every visitor has to try is stout, a strongish black beer with a creamy white head. Murphy's is brewed in Cork, but the most famous stout is Guinness, which has been brewed in Dublin since 1759. Great care is taken in serving it; about half a glass is poured and left to 'settle' for several minutes, then topped with the trademark creamy head. In a good Irish pub it will taste smooth as velvet, bearing no relation to the Guinness served in Britain or America.

Irish Whiskey

It is spelt differently from Scotch 'whisky' and tastes different too, as it is distilled from a mixture of malted and unmalted barley grains. The most popular brands are Bushmills, Jameson and Paddy, and all have a slightly different flavour. The fine old single malts are generally taken neat or with a splash of water as a digestif. Irish whiskey is also used in Irish coffee, a hot, sweet coffee spiked with whiskey and topped with cream, a delicious way to end a meal.

Above from far left:
fine dining at Brasserie One in Limerick; coffee the Irish way and the Italian way; Irish oatmeal fishcake; Italian café in Dublin.

Hot Whiskey
If you have been too long in the cold outdoors, there is no better cure than a hot whiskey, ideally sipped in front of an open fire. The bartender should dissolve a teaspoon of sugar in about an inch of boiling hot water, adding a slice of lemon studded with cloves and, of course, a measure of whiskey. Add more hot water to taste, and feel the warmth spreading to the very core of your being.

SHOPPING

Shopping in the two capitals is a pleasant experience, as both have compact centres. Designers use Irish wool and tweeds in high-fashion lines, while traditional craftmakers offer heirloom quality in glass, ceramics, linen and wool.

Both Dublin and Belfast have lively shopping areas, with a mix of department stores, high-street chains and quirky boutiques. In addition, there are shops that sell primarily Irish-made fashion and homewares, which attract Irish buyers as well as visitors. Cork, Limerick and Galway, and smaller towns like Kilkenny, Waterford and Tralee, have shops within the historic centres, so you can combine cultural tourism with retail therapy. Outside the cities, look out for craft shops and galleries with jewellery, leather, ceramics, glass, candles and prints.

DUBLIN

Shops north of the river are generally less fashionable but better value than those to the south. British-owned stores Marks & Spencer, Debenhams and Boots are prevalent. Ireland's version of Marks & Spencer is Dunnes Stores, while Irish chain Penney's (Primark in the UK) is the place for bargain versions of the latest fashions. Brown Thomas on Grafton Street is the most up-market department store; it also has branches in Cork, Limerick and Galway.

North of the River

O'Connell Street is home to Clerys, founded in 1853 as one of the world's first purpose-built department stores. From O'Connell Street, Henry Street runs past the famous Moore Street Market, where colourful characters sell fruit and vegetables with razor-sharp patter. It leads to the Ilac Centre, a large shopping mall, and the Jervis Centre, the newest mall, with the recently revamped Arnotts department store (the nearest tram (Luas) stop is Jervis).

South of the River

No doubt about it, the pedestrianised Grafton Street that runs from Trinity College south to St Stephen's Green, is a great deal of fun and is renowned for its buskers. Do not miss the Powerscourt Townhouse Centre to the west, an 18th-century mansion converted into a stylish shopping complex, and the massive glass-roofed Stephen's Green Shopping Centre (with an enormous branch of Dunnes). Grafton Street is a haven for high-street fashion; check out A-Wear, the Irish equivalent of Topshop, which offers catwalk-inspired fashion at low prices.

Opening Times
Most shops are open Monday to Saturday from 9am to 6pm. Many city centre shops stay open until 8 or 9pm on Thursday and Friday, and some of the bigger city-centre shops and suburban malls open on Sundays from noon to 6pm. In Belfast the main shopping centres stay open until at least 7pm in the week, and 6pm at weekends (although they do not open until 1pm on Sundays). There are several 24-hour supermarkets in Dublin, Cork, Limerick, Galway and Belfast.

To the west and northwest of Grafton Street, moving towards Temple Bar, you will find streetwear stores and music shops. Nassau Street near Trinity College has branches of the Blarney Woolen Mills and the Kilkenny Shop (Irish crafts and design), and there is a large branch of Avoca Handweavers in Suffolk Street. For Irish ladies' fashion, go to the first floor of Brown Thomas. Nassau Street, Dawson Street and Duke Street are rich in bookshops.

CORK, LIMERICK, GALWAY & SLIGO

Patrick Street is Cork city's mainstream shopping area, with more interesting boutiques, bookshops and galleries in Paul Street. Limerick's main drag is O'Connell Street; just off it is lively, pedestrianised Cruises Street. Besides its long main street, Galway has two large shopping malls near Eyre Square for more everyday stuff. Recently revamped Sligo town has an impressive new shopping centre, the Quayside, between Lower Quay Street and Wine Street.

BELFAST

Belfast has a bewildering choice of shops and, since you pay in sterling, they are often much better value than their southern neighbours. The most recent addition is the Victoria Square shopping centre, with its flagship House of Fraser department store, but Royal Avenue and the CastleCourt Centre are also worth a visit. Meanwhile, Botanic Avenue and the Queen's Quarter are filled with quirky bookshops, organic delis and vintage fashion boutiques. The Lisburn Road, to the south, is the destination for designer clothes and chichi home stores.

WHAT TO BUY

Hand-made crafts are expensive, and you will want to spend some time over your decision, but that is part of the fun. Shop around as you travel, comparing prices and quality. Kilkenny is a good place to start; Kilkenny Design Centre opposite the castle will give you a good idea of the high quality and scope of what is on offer, such as hand-made ceramics, hand-loomed mohair or alpaca blankets, fine linen that will last a lifetime and crystal glass, traditionally cut or in modern designs (Jerpoint Glass is superb). Irish-made jewellery also comes in traditional styles (the Claddagh ring, for example, *see p. 76*). Then there are sweaters and other knitted goods that make good presents. Tweed is made in Connemara and Donegal, and you can still buy hand-knitted sweaters on the Aran Islands, with a label naming the knitter. As well as Kilkenny, you will find a good range of craft shops in Avoca, Blarney, Kinsale, Kenmare, Dingle, Clifden and Westport.

Above from far left: Irish whiskey; hand-woven wool; traditional baskets.

Artisan Foods

Hand-made farmhouse cheeses, vacuum-packed smoked salmon and hand-made chocolates (Butlers is an Irish favourite), plus mustards, jams and traditional chutneys all make popular gifts. Then there are Irish whiskeys (Bushmills, Jameson), Irish stouts (Guinness, Murphy's and Beamish) and Irish-coffee liqueurs, the original being Baileys.

ENTERTAINMENT

Ireland's reputation as an easy-going party-loving nation enhances a packed calendar of arts and music festivals. Dublin is the theatre capital, while traditional music and dance can be found in every corner of the land.

The unexpected success of the Wexford Festival Opera – where international stars attracted large audiences to a small port in southeast Ireland, performing lesser-known operas in the dank Irish October – inspired an ambitious annual calendar of festivals and events. As in Wexford, these provide a buzz for the local community, with plenty of free entertainment, while also attracting visitors and boosting the local economy. While Ireland continues to maintain a high profile internationally in the literary and theatrical world, it also has the dubious kudos of being the originator of one of the world's most successful dance spectaculars, *Riverdance* (1994), responsible for making Irish dancing sexy. For entertainment and nightlife listings, *see pp.122–3*.

Festivals

The festival season opens with Dublin's five-day celebration of Saint Patrick's Day on 17 March. It was originally introduced because so many visitors were disappointed to find that, unlike the shenanigans abroad, nothing much happened in Ireland on the great day.

Festivals are now a key element in Ireland's entertainment scene. An Irish festival often goes on for a 10-day 'week', including weekends, and aims to entertain all, from children to the elderly. You never know who you will find headlining the list of attractions: a 'local' like Van Morrison or Sinead O'Connor, or a big-name guest from the shores beyond. Cork Midsummer Festival (June), Galway Arts Festival (July), Kilkenny Arts Festival (August) and Belfast Festival at Queen's (October) are among the biggest general artsfests. Popular newcomers include the Street Performance World Championships in Dublin and Cork (June), the Dun Laoghaire Festival of World Cultures (August) and Galway's Baboró International Arts Festival for Children (October). There are also specialist festivals for classical music and traditional music (known as *fleadh*), and literary festivals galore.

THEATRE

Ever since the Abbey Theatre's production of *The Playboy of the Western World* by John M. Synge in 1907 caused a famous riot (people reacted violently to its use of the word 'shift', referring to a female undergarment), Dublin has had an exciting theatre scene. It also offers great value for money, with tickets at the Abbey starting at €18, often available at short notice. Productions from the Gate Theatre, which fostered the work of Brian Friel, regularly transfer to New York.

Belfast, Wexford, Kilkenny, Waterford, Cork, Galway and Sligo all have

well-equipped theatres that host touring productions and sometimes produce their own too. Galway's Druid Theatre Company has successfully transferred productions to Broadway, such as Martin McDonagh's *The Cripple of Inishman*.

Language is no barrier at Siamsa Tire, Ireland's National Folk Theatre (Town Park, Tralee, Co. Kerry; tel: 066-712 3055; www.siamsatire.com). The titles of the plays are Irish, and the themes are based on Celtic myth and folklore, but the performances are energetic spectaculars, featuring music, song, dance and mime, with no dialogue.

DANCE

Before *Riverdance* burst on to the scene, very few traditional Irish dancers made a living by toe-tapping. Now touring productions are in great demand, and can also be seen in Irish cabaret at places like Bunratty Castle. The best way to enjoy Irish dance is to join in a set dancing session; these are like the barn or square dances. Set dancing sessions take place in pubs and community halls, and newcomers are usually welcomed and taught a few steps.

MUSIC

Wherever you travel in Ireland you will encounter live traditional music, most often in a pub. A gathering of traditional musicians on an informal, unpaid basis is known as a *seisiún* (ses-

sion), and creates its own momentum, as musicians improvise and take flight. Many publicans employ musicians to entertain their customers from about 10pm, and the music is usually free.

NIGHTLIFE

Dublin has over 120 clubs and live-music pubs. The club scene is mainly for the under 30s, who flock to the city from all over Europe in search of a good time. In the rest of the Republic, nightlife is generally an extension of the pub scene; quite literally, as certain pubs in each town are regularly granted a special licence, known as an extension, to stay open until 2am. Ask locally.

In Belfast you can find traditional city-centre music venues, a burgeoning bar scene in the Cathedral Quarter and shabby-chic music clubs in the student areas of the south.

Above from far left: Dublin's nightlife scene centres on Temple Bar; traditional *bodhrán* drums; Irish dancing; Olympia Theatre in Dublin.

Below: fiddling at a live music venue in Belfast.

OUTDOOR ACTIVITIES

Ireland has long been a destination for lovers of the outdoors. Initially attracting golfers and anglers, its easily accessible wilderness areas now lure walkers, climbers and cyclists, while its beaches have been discovered by surfers.

Ireland's golf courses continue to be a major magnet for visitors, its traditional links courses now joined by major new developments, such as the Jack Nicklaus-designed course at Mount Juliet. Meanwhile, game, coarse and sea anglers continue to be hooked by Ireland's network of lakes and rivers and long coastline. Walkers are catered for by a range of looped and waymarked walks, cyclists can follow sign-posted trails and surfers can make the most of the Atlantic swell on much of the north, west and south coasts. For specific details on all the activities mentioned below, check the Failte Ireland website: www.discoverireland.ie.

GOLFING

Ireland has over 400 courses around the island, including over 30 percent of the world's natural links courses. The Irish are keen golfers, and it is generally seen as an accessible sport of the people, rather than a status symbol. The majority of Irish clubs are unstuffy places that welcome visitors, who are usually pleasantly surprised at the low price of green fees. Exceptions to this are the more expensive parkland courses at the K-Club, Adare Manor and Mount Juliet, and some of the more famous links courses like Lahinch and Waterville.

ANGLING

The infrastructure of angling centres and boat operators has improved greatly in recent years. Alas, at the same time, water quality has declined in rivers and lakes all over Ireland,

Gaelic Games

Hurling and Gaelic football arouse such passions in Ireland that they are often described as a religion. These are fast-paced, high-voltage games, played by dedicated amateurs, organised around the parish and controlled by the Gaelic Athletic Association (GAA). Hurling is played with a wooden hurley, which can propel the ball along the ground, carry the ball aloft on its paddle-like extreme or throw it in the air. It is said to be one of the fastest ball games in the world, and is certainly one of the most exciting to watch. Gaelic football, like hurling, is played by teams of 15-a-side, on the same size pitch, with a round, soccer-sized ball. It has similarities with rugby and association football, but throwing is not allowed. The main season runs from early summer, and culminates in the All-Ireland finals in Dublin's Croke Park in late September. For fixtures, see www.gaa.ie.

with the excessive input of nutrients being the main cause of the trouble. While the old-timers will tell you that the fishing is not what it used to be, Ireland continues to be a popular destination for game, coarse and sea angling.

WALKING

There are now 43 long-distance way-marked walking routes, and a network of shorter looped walks, designed so that you return to your starting point within one to three hours. It is easy to escape the crowds in such a sparsely populated country, and you can be walking in impressively wild, uninhabited scenery within an hour or less of landing at the airport. To find a nearby walk see www.irishtrails.ie

CYCLING

Certain towns, such as Wesport, Achill, Skibbereen and Clifden have been designated 'cycling hubs', as they provide good accommodation and eating options, along with a choice of looped cycling routes suitable for all fitness levels. Organised cycling holidays are increasingly popular, either travelling in a group with a back-up van, or cycling independently to pre-booked accommodation, with baggage transfer. There are also designated mountain bike parks on forest tracks in rural areas for adrenaline addicts.

HORSE-RIDING

Ireland rears some of the world's finest horses, from million-dollar racehorses to good-natured, long-haired ponies. Whether you choose a residential riding holiday with tuition on a challenging cross-country course, or a pleasant amble around quiet lanes on a hairy pony, be honest about your abilities, so that the stable can match you with the right horse.

ADVENTURE CENTRES

Learn sea-kayaking, canoeing, orienteering, rock climbing, abseiling and other outdoor skills at the fast-growing network of outdoor adventure centres. Send the kids, or book a guided family day out.

SURFING

Beaches used to be empty in bad weather, except for a few dog walkers. Now they are busy whatever the weather, with kitesurfers, windsurfers and, most numerous of all, surfers. A wet suit is essential, but it is a rare day when you will not find a rideable wave on the west coast. Surf schools offer tuition to beginners on the more benign beach breaks, while the more advanced surfers are towed out by jet-ski, hoping to catch the famous Aileens beneath the Cliffs of Mohor, some of Europe's biggest waves at over 25 feet – awesome!

The Maharees
The Maharees is a 5km (3 mile) tombolo (sand spit) that divides Brandon Bay and Tralee Bay in County Kerry. Surfers delight in the Atlantic waves on the long sandy beaches, while the Maharees Islands attract sea anglers and divers. There's a 19km (12 mile) stretch of the Dingle Way (see p.64) parallel to the beach on Brandon Bay, where horse-riding is also an option (O'Connor's Trekking; tel: 066-713 9216).

HISTORY: KEY DATES

Ireland has changed from a traditional post-colonial society into a secular Europe-oriented state, and is now weathering the transition from economic boom to almost-bust. But boom or bust, the Irish proudly maintain their reputation for knowing how to enjoy themselves.

EARLY PERIOD

*c.*7,000BC	Date of the earliest archaeological evidence found along the coast.
500BC	Celts migrate to Britain. Ireland's Iron Age begins.
432AD	St Patrick arrives as a missionary.
500–800	Early monasticism; Ireland becomes a European centre of learning.
9th century	The Vikings invade, founding Dublin.
1014	Brian Ború, King of Munster, defeats the Vikings.

ENGLISH CONQUEST

1169	The Anglo-Normans conquer large areas of the island.
1541	Henry VIII declares himself King of Ireland.
1556	Protestant settlers arrive from England and Scotland.
1649–50	The rebellion of Irish Catholics is crushed by Oliver Cromwell.
1690	The Battle of the Boyne is won by William of Orange, and Protestant rule begins.
1691	The Irish-Protestant parliament introduces the 'Penal Laws' denying Catholics the right to hold public office, own property or vote.

FREEDOM STRUGGLES

1798	Wolfe Tone's Rebellion, backed by French armed forces, is crushed by the British; some 30,000 die.
1801	Ireland incorporated into the United Kingdom by the Act of Union.
1829	Daniel O'Connell ('the Liberator') achieves Catholic Emancipation.
1845–9	The Great Potato Famine results in the deaths of around 1 million and the emigration of 1 million more.
1858	The Irish Republican Brotherhood, forerunner of the IRA, is founded.
1875	Charles Stewart Parnell is elected MP; leads Home Rule movement.

Newgrange

Newgrange (see www.newgrange.com for visiting details), a large Neolithic tomb in the Boyne Valley near Drogheda north of Dublin, looks like a man-made hilltop, but is in fact an amazing feat of prehistoric engineering and one of Europe's best examples of a passage-grave. The narrow tunnel leading to the central shrine is positioned to let the sun shine in on the shortest day of the year, 21 December. At its end you can stand in the circular vault and look up at the ceiling to see the remarkable 5,000-year-old technique used in its construction. There are two more Neolithic tumuli at nearby Knowth and Dowth.

| 1885 | Home Rule is defeated in the House of Lords. |
| 1905–12 | The struggle over Home Rule intensifies with the formation of armed militias, including the Ulster Volunteer Force. |

INDEPENDENCE & AFTER

1916	The Easter Rising is defeated, the leaders executed and martial law imposed.
1918	Sinn Féin wins the general election, boycotts the House of Commons and elects the jailed Eamonn de Valera as president.
1919	British anti-terrorist forces – the 'Black and Tans' – attacked by IRA.
1921	Britain and Ireland sign a treaty granting 'Dominion' status to Ireland. The six counties of Ulster remain in UK.
1922–3	Civil war between pro- and anti-partitionists.
1939–45	During World War II the Irish Free State remains neutral.
1949	The Free State leaves the Commonwealth and becomes a Republic.

NORTH & SOUTH RECONCILE

1969	A civil rights dispute in Northern Ireland leads to the armed struggle known as 'The Troubles'.
1973	Ireland joins the European Community (now the European Union).
1990	Mary Robinson is elected the Republic's first woman president.
1998	All parties sign the Northern Ireland peace treaty known as the Good Friday Agreement.
1999	An all-party assembly with limited powers is set up in Northern Ireland.
2002	The Republic adopts the euro. In the North, direct rule from London is reimposed.
2003	Elections in Northern Ireland restore the all-party assembly.

BOOM TO BUST

2004	Ireland's economic boom, nicknamed the Celtic Tiger, is at its peak.
2005	The IRA says its war is over, its weapons destroyed.
2008	After controversy over his finances, Ahern resigns, and his deputy, Brian Cowen assumes leadership.
2011	Landslide victory for Enda Kenny's Fine Gael party after years in opposition. Socialist and poet Michael D. Higgins elected President.

Above from far left: the Carrowmore Megalithic Cemetery in County Sligo is dotted with ancient tombs; memorial service and procession for soldiers of the Irish Free State Army during the Irish Civil War.

The Irish Flag
In the predominantly nationalist Republic, the flag was referred to in song as 'green, white and gold'. The gold portion is in fact orange, representing the 'Orange' allegiances of Northern Protestants (dating from the Battle of the Boyne in 1690), while the green stands for the nationalist aspirations of Irish Catholics, and the white centre stripe is thought to symbolise peace between the two.

WALKS & TOURS

HISTORIC DUBLIN

This full-day walk covers the main historic sights of Dublin, skirting the banks of the River Liffey and taking in the medieval centre, Trinity College and Temple Bar, one of the oldest – and liveliest – parts of the city.

DISTANCE 5.25km (3¼ miles)
TIME A full day
START Four Courts
END Clarence Hotel, Temple Bar
POINTS TO NOTE
To reach the starting point, take the tram (Luas) to the Four Courts stop, just behind the Four Courts Building.
   If you intend to visit most or all of the sights on this walk, consider buying a Dublin Pass. The pass will give you free entry to most major Dublin attractions (see www.dublinpass.ie for details of where you can buy this).
   On Sundays Dublin Castle is only open in the afternoon.

Viking Splash Tours
Exploring the main sights of Dublin on land and water in an amphibious craft, these tours end up by 'splashing' into the the newly developed Grand Canal Basin. The regular departure point is at St Stephen's Green North; you can buy tickets (adults: €20, children 12 and under: €10) by phone (01-707 6000), online (www.vikingsplash.ie) or from any Dublin Tourism Centre.

Although Mesolithic and Neolithic peoples occupied settlements in the area in the 8th century BC, it was not until the Vikings arrived in the 9th century AD that Dublin first came into existence. In the winter of 841 the Vikings settled on the banks of the River Liffey. Following the Anglo-Norman invasion of 1169, the Normans built Dublin Castle, and the cathedrals of St Patrick and Christchurch. This walk begins in the very area where the Vikings and later the Normans set down their roots in Dublin.

FOUR COURTS

Begin at the **Four Courts ❶** on Inns Quay, on the northern side of the river. Notable for its large dome and portico, the building was designed between 1796 and 1802 by James Gandon (who also designed the Custom House, further east down the river, and the Bank of Ireland). The name is derived from the four divisions that traditionally constituted the Irish judicial system: Chancery, King's Bench, Exchequer and Common Pleas; this remains the main courts building for the Irish Republic.

Cross over the Liffey at the **Father Matthew Bridge**. Looking left towards the city centre, the southern riverbank leads from Merchants Quay to Wood Quay, the site of the first Viking settlement in what is now the city centre. The settlement was actually sited on the River Poddle, a tributary of the Liffey; however, it was covered up in the late 1700s and largely forgotten.

SOUTH OF THE RIVER

Crossing onto Bridge Street, you will pass the **Brazen Head**, which claims to be Ireland's oldest pub (established in 1198). From here the road bends left to meet Cornmarket, where you will pass the two **churches of St Audoen**: on the left, the 19th-century Catholic church; on the right, a Church of Ireland edifice, built in 1190. The latter, Dublin's only surviving medieval church, is thought to be the oldest of its kind in Ireland. Facing them is the **Tailors' Hall** (1706), Dublin's only remaining guildhall.

St Patrick's Cathedral

Continuing along Cornmarket onto High Street, a right turn takes you down Nicholas Street to **St Patrick's Cathedral ②** (St Patrick's Close; tel: 01-453 9472; www.stpatrickscathedral. ie; Mon–Fri 9am–5pm, Nov–Feb Sun 9–10.30am, 12.30–2.30pm, Mar–Oct Sat 9am–6pm, Sun 12.30–2.30pm, 4.30–6pm; charge). A church has stood here since the 5th century, while legend has it that St Patrick baptised converts at a well in the churchyard. The present cathedral was built by the Normans and restored in the mid-19th century; particularly impressive are the enormous flying buttresses that support the magnificent roof. Jonathan Swift, the Dublin-born author of *Gulliver's Travels* and master of prose satire, was Dean here between 1714 and 1745. The well-manicured cathedral gardens are free to visit.

Above from far left: Four Courts dome; St Patrick's.

Baile Átha Cliath

The modern Irish Gaelic name for Dublin, 'Baile Átha Cliath', first recorded in 1368, translates as 'Town of the Ford of the Reed Hurdles'. It refers to a fording point of the Liffey near Heuston Station, to the west of Father Matthew Bridge.

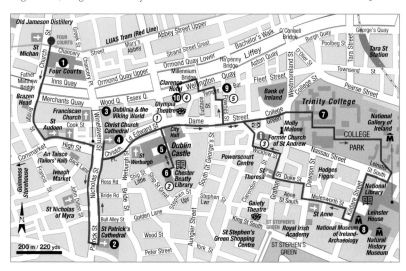

Above from left:
Dublin Castle; door
knocker, Christ
Church Cathedral;
castle detail; tiled
floor of the cathedral.

Christchurch Place

Retrace your steps along Nicholas Street to **Dublinia and the Viking World ❸** (St Michael's Hill; tel: 01-679 4611; www.dublinia.ie; daily 10am–5pm, last entry 4.15pm; charge), just past High Street on the left. Reconstructions of medieval street scenes, gory exhibitions of medieval medicine and torture, and interactive presentations of Viking life, will keep kids entertained for hours.

Opposite are the gardens of **Christ Church Cathedral ❹** (Christchurch Place; tel: 01-677 8099; www.cccdub.ie; Mon–Sat 9.45am–4.15pm, Sun 12.30–2.30pm, later times in summer; charge). Begun in about 1030, Christchurch is the only cathedral of Norse foundation in Ireland or Britain. It was rebuilt in Norman times and remodelled in the 1870s. Highlights include the beautiful tiled floor and the 11th-century crypt, the oldest structure in Dublin.

At the end of Christchurch Place, cross over Werburgh Street and take the left of the two facing roads – Lord Edward Street. At the point at which Lord Edward Street meets Dame Street, a right turn just before the **City Hall** (built in 1769) will take you to Cork Hill, and the bright red façade of **The Queen of Tarts**, see ⑪①, one of the city's best cafés.

DUBLIN CASTLE

Cork Hill Gate is the official entrance to **Dublin Castle ❺** (Castle Street; tel: 01-645 8813; www.dublincastle.ie; Mon–Sat 10am–4.45pm, Sun and hols noon–4.45pm; grounds free; entrance to State apartments by 45-min guided tour only; charge). Historical evidence suggests that a Danish Viking fortress was built here in around 930AD. The Normans built a wood-and-stone castle in the 1170s; then, between 1204 and 1230, King John erected a larger, stronger castle on the same site. Unfortunately, most of the medieval castle, except for the southeastern tower, was destroyed by fire in 1684. As it stands today, the majority of the castle dates from the Georgian era. Tours of the castle take in the grand State Apart-

Drinkers' Dublin

You can sample two of Ireland's most famous exports at locations near the city centre. The Guinness Brewery, 1km (⅔ mile) to the west, is the biggest brewery in Europe, producing 2½ million pints of Guinness every day. The Guinness Storehouse (Thomas Street; tel: 01-408 4800; www.guinnessstorehouse. com; daily 9.30am–5pm, July and Aug 9.30am–7pm; charge) showcases the making and history of the world-famous stout. Admission entitles you to a complimentary pint in the Gravity Bar, the highest in Dublin, with panoramic views over the city.

Alternatively, the Old Jameson Distillery (Bow Street; tel: 01-807 2355; www.tours.jamesonhiskey. com; continuous tours 9am–5.15pm; charge) is housed in the old warehouse of the 1791 whiskey factory.

ments, the Gothic-Revivalist Chapel Royal and the fascinating Undercroft, the point at which the city walls join the castle below ground.

Follow the signs through the castle grounds to the **Castle Gardens**, site of the first 'pool' of the city – the 'Dubh-linn' ('black pool') from which the city derives its name. The Vikings would moor their ships at this spot, where the River Poddle 'pooled'.

Chester Beatty Library

Continuing through the Castle Gardens takes you to the magnificently quirky **Chester Beatty Library** ⑥ (Dublin Castle; tel: 01-407 0750; www.cbl.ie; Mon–Fri 10am–5pm, Sat 11am–5pm, Sun 1–5pm, Oct–Apr closed Mon; free). Permanent exhibitions, taken from the extensive collections of the American mining magnate and art patron Sir Alfred Chester Beatty (1875–1968), include Islamic, Christian, Jewish and Buddhist manuscripts, printed texts, religious artefacts and artworks. There is also a pleasant roof garden, a reading room and a bookshop. The excellent **Silk Road Café**, see ⑪②, in the atrium on the ground floor, echoes the museum's eastern leanings.

TRINITY COLLEGE

Leave the castle grounds by Cork Hill Gate and turn right onto Dame Street, which leads straight down to **College Green**, a popular meeting spot.

College Green faces the 18th-century **Bank of Ireland**, completed in 1785 by James Gandon (open during banking hours). A **statue of Henry Grattan** (1746–1820), the Irish parliament's greatest orator, stands in the middle of the green.

Trinity College ⑦ was founded in 1592 by Elizabeth I on the site of a confiscated monastery. The Front Gate, however, was built between 1755 and 1759. Passing through it, you will reach the cobbled quadrangle of **Parliament Square**, with its tall (30m/100ft) campanile, designed by Sir Charles Lanyon and erected in 1853. On the right-hand side of Parliament Square is a little

Old Trinitarians

Established by Elizabeth I to educate the Protestant Ascendancy class, Trinity College has educated a host of Anglo-Irish cultural figures. Famous alumni include the historian and statesman Edmund Burke, writer Oliver Goldsmith, and poet Thomas Moore, and more recently Oscar Wilde, playwright J.M. Synge and Bram Stoker, author of *Dracula*.

Food & Drink

① QUEEN OF TARTS
Cork Hill, Dame Street; tel: 01-670 7499; daily 8am–7pm, Sun 10am–6pm; €
Outstandingly good tarts, sweet and savoury, salads, sandwiches and delicious cakes, all in a relaxing atmosphere.

② SILK ROAD CAFÉ
Chester Beatty Library; tel: 01-407 0770; Mon–Fri 10am–4.30pm, Sat 11am–4.30pm, Sun 1–4.30pm, Oct–May closed Mon; €–€€
This bright café serves up a mouth-watering selection of Greek and Middle-Eastern specials (such as koftes and moussaka) and an impressive selection of fresh salads.

③ CORNUCOPIA
19–20 Wicklow Street; tel: 01-677 7583; www.cornucopia.ie; Mon–Tue 8.30am–9pm, Wed–Sat 8.30am–10.15pm Sun noon–9pm; €
Generations of Trinity students have refuelled at this wholesome vegetarian restaurant where the generous portions of tasty fare recall the best home-cooking. Excellent breakfast.

National Library

Those with an interest in Irish literature should visit the National Library of Ireland (Kildare Street; tel: 01-603 0200; www.nli.ie; Mon–Wed 9.30am–7.45pm, Thur–Fri until 4.45pm, Sat until 12.45pm; free; exhibitions as above plus Sun 1pm–5pm; free). The library's intelligently presented changing exhibitions draw on its vast resources; look out for manuscripts, letters and first editions of Irish writers such as W.B. Yeats or James Joyce.

Below: floor mosaics at the National Museum of Ireland.

booth from where you can buy tickets for student-led tours of the College, including the Old Library and the *Book of Kells*.

Trinity College Library

Leaving Parliament Square by the top right corner, you will find (on your left) the entrance to **Trinity College Library** and the *Book of Kells* (tel 01-896 1171; www.tcd.ie/library; Mon–Sat 9.30am–5pm, Oct–May Sun noon–4.30pm, June–Sept Sun 9.30am–4.30pm; charge). The *Book of Kells*, probably produced early in the 9th century by the monks of Iona, is one of the most beautifully illuminated manuscripts in the world. Its vellum pages contain the four Gospels in Latin, each one decorated with intricate painted illustrations. The manuscript was given to Trinity College in the 17th century.

The **Old Library** (1712–32) contains the magnificent **Long Room**. Its high windows let in shafts of glorious light, which rest upon the high bookcases and on the busts of literary and artistic figures that flank them. Changing exhibitions from the library's collections are accompanied by a permanent display of one of the dozen remaining copies of the 1916 'Proclamation of the Irish Republic' *(see also feature, p.36)*.

Leaving the Old Library, turn left to enter the delightful **College Park**. Passing the cricket pavilion on your right, a right turn takes you to the southeastern exit of Trinity College.

KILDARE STREET & DAWSON STREET

Turning right out of Trinity along Leinster Street South and taking the first left, will bring you to Kildare Street, home of some of the most important buildings in Dublin. The first you will pass is the **National Library of Ireland** (1890) on your left *(see margin, left)*. Next door is **Leinster House** (1746), seat of the two Oíreachtas (Houses of Parliament), the Dáil and the Seanad (Irish Parliament and Senate).

National Museum of Ireland

Like the National Library, the **National Museum of Ireland – Archaeology** ❽ (Kildare Street; tel: 01-677 7444; www.museum.ie; Tue–Sat 10am–5pm, Sun 2–5pm; free) has a columnar entrance rotunda and was constructed in 1890. Its archaeological exhibitions trace the development of Irish civilisation from the Mesolithic or Middle Stone Age to Late Medieval Ireland; separate exhibitions also showcase artefacts from ancient Egypt and Cyprus. A visit to the museum is highly recommended, if only to marvel at its richly decorated interior.

Literary Dublin

Leaving Kildare Street west via Molesworth Street brings you to Dawson Street, home of the excellent **Hodges Figgis Bookshop** (56–8 Dawson Street; tel: 01-677 4754). This elegant building contains an excellent selection

of Irish literature and has a well-stocked 'bargain basement'; meanwhile, **Cathach Books** (tel: 01-671 8676; www.rare books.ie), selling rare books, prints and maps of Irish interest, can be found on nearby **Duke Street**, also the home of Dublin's famous literary pub crawl *(see margin, right)*.

Duke Street leads to the pedestrian shopping area of **Grafton Street** *(see pp.18 and 37)*. A right turn takes you back towards College Green. Take the first left down **Wicklow Street**, to recharge your batteries with a tasty vegetarian treat at **Cornucopia**, see ⑪③ *(see p.31)*. Turn right from here and follow the bend into St Andrew Street to return to Dame Street.

TEMPLE BAR

Take any right turn off Dame Street (such as Fownes Street) to reach lively and chaotic **Temple Bar ❾**. The area is named after Sir William Temple, who acquired the land in the early 1600s; by the early 1700s it had become a place of ill repute, full of pubs and prostitutes. Today's Temple Bar still has the pubs, but the prostitutes have been replaced by artists, musicians and film-makers: the entire area was redeveloped when Dublin was chosen as the 1991 European City of Culture.

Head through busy streets, avoiding the ubiquitous hen and stag parties, to arrive at the River Liffey, which is dyed green every year to celebrate St Patrick's

day (17 March). To the right is the white cast-iron arc of the 1816 **Ha'penny Bridge** (officially, the Liffey Bridge), one of Dublin's best-loved landmarks. The less exciting **Millennium Bridge**, to its left, joins Eustace Street in Temple Bar to the north quays.

On the south bank, west of the Millennium Bridge, is Wellington Quay, home of the **Clarence Hotel ❿**. Owned by Bono and the Edge from U2, the Clarence is the landmark building of Temple Bar. Built in 1852 and refurbished in Art Deco style, it stands on the site of Dublin's original Customs House. The Clarence's **Octagon Bar**, see ⑪④, is great for people watching over a pre-dinner cocktail. For dinner, a restaurant with a claim to fame of its own – Sinead O'Connor was once a waitress there – is nearby **Bad Ass Café**, see ⑪⑤.

Above from far left: on the shelves at the Hodges Figgis Bookshop; Trinity College; Temple Bar graffiti.

Literary Pub Crawl The Dublin Literary Pub Crawl (www. dublinpubcrawl.com) starts at The Duke on Duke Street. Many writers have propped up the bar there, while Leopold Bloom, anti-hero of Joyce's *Ulysses*, enjoyed a gorgonzola sandwich and a glass of burgundy at Davy Byrne's.

Food & Drink 🍽️

④ OCTAGON BAR AT THE CLARENCE HOTEL

6–8 Wellington Quay; tel: 01-407 0800 (hotel reception); Tue–Thur 5–11.30pm, Fri–Sat 5pm–12.30am
This octagon-shaped, honey-coloured bar is the place to see and be seen in Dublin. The cocktails (€6–15) are world-class and excellent value. Try the flavoured daiquiris or the delicious 'Bramble' (a gin-based cocktail).

⑤ BAD ASS CAFÉ

9–11 Crown Alley; tel: 01-671 2596; daily 11.30am–late; €–€€
This Dublin institution is as famous for its burgers – try the 'Posh' or the 'California' – as it is for its unique pulley ordering system. It also serves up huge breakfasts, pizzas (including a mighty calzone), salads and pastas.

MODERN DUBLIN

Modern Dublin was shaped by its writers, artists and thinkers. This walk covers the literary, political and artistic sights of the city – from the Dublin Writers Museum to the General Post Office to the National Gallery of Ireland – to illustrate how Dublin became the culturally vibrant capital it is today.

DISTANCE 4km (2½ miles)
TIME A full day
START Parnell Square
END National Gallery of Ireland
POINTS TO NOTE
Many city-centre buses pass close to the beginning of the walk. Alternatively, Parnell Square is a 10-minute walk from Connolly and Tara Street DART stations, and a 5-minute walk north from the Abbey Street tram (Luas) stop.
   Note that Bewley's Café Theatre is closed on Sundays.

Food & Drink

① BRAMBLES CAFÉ
Dublin City Gallery The Hugh Lane, Charlemont House, Parnell Square North; Tue–Thur 10am–5.30pm, Fri–Sun 10am–4.30pm; €
This bright and airy café serves delicious cakes and pastries, deli-style sandwiches and light meals. Licensed.

This walk moves from north to south, taking in the inspirational museums of Parnell Square as well as the political and historical monuments of O'Connell Street and O'Connell Bridge, and passing into the fashionable southern side of the city, with its elegant shopping arcades, green spaces and impressive Georgian architecture.

PARNELL SQUARE

Tranquil **Parnell Square**, one of Dublin's five Georgian squares, is home to the **Garden of Remembrance** ❶ (Mon–Sat 8.30am–7.30pm, Sun 10am–6pm; free). Established in 1966 to commemorate the 50th anniversary of the 1916 Easter Rising

Right: Dublin Writers Museum exhibits.

(see feature, p.36), it is dedicated to the memory of all those who gave their lives for the cause of Irish freedom.

Dublin Writers Museum

Since 2010 Dublin has been designated a Unesco City of Literature in recognition of its literary heritage,

A fine Georgian house on the north side of Parnell Square is home to the **Dublin Writers Museum** ❷ (18 Parnell Square; tel: 01-872 2077; www. writersmuseum.com; Mon–Sat 10am–5pm, Sun 11am–5pm; charge). The museum charts the history of Irish writing from its roots in poetry and storytelling to the 20th century, covering Oscar Wilde, George Bernard Shaw, W.B. Yeats, James Joyce *(see also margin)* and Samuel Beckett.

Dublin City Gallery
The Hugh Lane

A few doors down, the dazzling **Dublin City Gallery The Hugh Lane** ❸ (tel: 01-222 5550; www.hughlane. ie; Tue–Thur 10am–6pm, Fri and Sat 10am–5pm, Sun 11am–5pm; free) houses modern and contemporary European and Irish artworks. Sir Hugh Lane (1875–1915) established Dublin's Municipal Gallery of Modern Art on Harcourt Street in 1908; the collection was moved here in 1933. There are some 2,000 works by artists such as Manet, Monet, Toulouse Lautrec and the 20th-century Irish painter (and brother of W.B. Yeats) Jack B. Yeats.

Since 2001 the museum has also been home to Francis Bacon's studio, reconstructed in its chaotic entirety. **Brambles Café**, see ⑪①, makes a pleasant stop for morning coffee.

O'CONNELL STREET

Retrace your steps, and turn right onto Parnell Square East. At the point at which Parnell Square East becomes Upper O'Connell Street stands the **Parnell Monument** ❹, designed by the American sculptor Augustus Saint-Gaudens and erected in 1903–7. The politician Charles Stewart Parnell (1846–91) became a national hero through his campaigns for Irish Home Rule. However in 1886, on being implicated in the divorce case of a married woman, Kitty O'Shea, he suffered a dramatic fall from grace. Parnell's legacy was famously debated in James Joyce's *A Portrait of the Artist as a Young Man* (1916) and *Dubliners* (1914).

Continuing south along O'Connell Street, the **Spire of Dublin** ❺ rises up as if from below ground. With the official title 'Monument of Light', the Spire was the winning entry in a 2002 architectural competition to provide a replacement for Nelson's Column, which was blown up on the site in 1966 by an IRA explosion. It is 120m (400ft) in height, and 3m (9ft) in diameter at the base, but only 15cm (6in) at the top. Nearby, on the corner with Earl Street North, is a fanciful statue of Joyce.

Joyce Centre
Fans may wish to make a detour to the James Joyce Centre (35 North Great George's Street; tel: 01-878 8547; www. jamesjoyce.ie; Tue–Sat 10am–5pm, Sun noon–5pm; charge), which showcases editions of Joyce's works, reconstructs his living quarters and displays some of his letters to Nora Barnacle, leaving out the seamier details of his life and loves. The Centre also organises lectures, 'Bloomsday' events (commemorating 16 June 1904, the day in which the events of *Ulysses* unfold) and walking tours of the city.

To get there, cross over Parnell Square East to Denmark Street and turn right down North Great George's Street. The centre is about 100m/yds down the hill on the left.

Above from left:
General Post Office;
Spire of Dublin;
Parnell Monument;
GPO clock.

Easter Rising

On Easter Monday (24 April) 1916, a motley group of armed nationalists seized control of buildings throughout Dublin. Standing on the steps of the GPO, the poet and playwright Padraig Pearse read out the 'Proclamation of the Irish Republic'. A bloody standoff ensued between British troops and nationalist insurgents, which lasted six days and left a lot of the city centre in ruins. In a much-criticised attempt to halt the insurgents' efforts, the British government arrested 3,430 men and 79 women, and executed 15 of the leaders, including Pearse. This action did much to inspire Irish nationalist feeling, and resentment: as W.B. Yeats put it in his poem 'Easter 1916', 'A terrible beauty is born'.

Abbey Theatre
A left turn off O'Connell Street takes you to the Abbey Theatre (26 Lower Abbey Street; tel: 01-8787 222; www.abbey theatre.ie; box office open Mon–Sat 10.30am–7pm), built in 1966 on the site of the original Abbey Theatre, established by W.B. Yeats, Lady Gregory and J.M. Synge in 1903 as part of the Celtic Revival. *See also p.122.*

Map labels

MONTJOY SQUARE

Dorset Street
Frederick St N.
Hill
Denmark Street
Gardiner Street Lower
Great Denmark Street

Dublin Writers Museum **2** **M**

Parnell Square N.
North Gt George's St.
James Joyce Cultural Centre
Rutland Pl. West
Parnell St.

Parnell Sq. East

1 GARDEN OF REMEMBRANCE

Parnell Monument **4**

Parnell Sq. West
3 **1**
Gate Theatre
Cathal Brugha St.

Dublin City Gallery The Hugh Lane
O'Connell Street Upper
Marlborough Street

Parnell St.
Moore St.
Henry St.
St Mary's Pro-Cathedral

Spire of Dublin **5**
Talbot St.

General Post Office **6**
Clerys
Abbey Theatre

Mary St.
Liffey St. Upper
ABBEY ST

LUAS Tram (Red Line)
Abbey Street Middle
Daniel O'Connell
Eden Quay

JERVIS
Lotts
7
O'Connell Bridge

Strand Street Gt.
Bachelor's Walk
Liffey

Ha'penny Bridge
Aston Quay
O'Dier St.

Millennium Bridge
Wellington Quay
Fleet Street
College St.

Temple Bar
Westmoreland St.

Olympia Theatre
Bank of Ireland
Trinity College

Dame Street
College Green

Former Church of St Andrew **1**
Melly Malone

Wicklow St.
Nassau

Powerscourt Centre
St Theresa
Rd
Leinster St.
Oscar Wilde House **6**
Fenian St.

South Great George's St.
Drury St.
Clarendon St.
William St. S.
Grafton Street
Duke Street
Anne St S.
Dawson Street
Molesworth St.
National Gallery of Ireland **13** **M**
Clare St.
Denzille Lane

2
Gaiety Theatre
St Anne
National Library
Leinster House
Natural History Museum **M**
Merrion Square North

King Street
ST STEPHEN'S GREEN
Royal Irish Academy
Kildare St.
National Museum of Ireland
MERRION SQUARE

St Stephen's Green Shopping Centre
St Stephen's Green West
St Stephen's Green North
Shelbourne Hotel
Government Buildings **10** **5**
Upper Merrion St.
Merrion Square South
Merrion Square E.
11

Aungier Street
York Street
Merrion Row

8
9
Ely Place
Fitzwilliam Lane

Mercer St. Up.
ST STEPHEN'S GREEN
Huguenot cemetery **3**
29 Lower Fitzwilliam Street **12**

Cuffe Street
St Stephen's Green South
St Stephen's Green East
Baggot Street

Wexford St.
University Church

N
300 m / 330 yds

General Post Office

The Palladian-style **General Post Office ❻** (www.anpost.ie/historyand heritage; tel: 01-705 7000; Mon–Sat 8am–8pm, Sun 10.30am–6.30pm; free), built in 1818, faces the spire on the western side of O'Connell Street. The GPO was the site of the reading of the 'Proclamation of the Irish Republic' on Easter Monday 1916 *(see feature, left)*. The bullet holes on its columns are a reminder of the bloody legacy of that day. Inside, the walls display a series of paintings commemorating the Rising. Almost opposite the GPO, Clerys department store, traditionally Dublin's best, is an excellent spot for some retail therapy.

Daniel O'Connell Monument

Continue south down O'Connell Street and the last statue that you pass is the **Daniel O'Connell monument ❼**. Known as the 'Liberator' *(see also feature, p.61)*, O'Connell (1775–1847)

campaigned for Catholic emancipation – the right for Catholics to sit at parliament in Westminster – and for the dissolution of the Act of Union between Ireland and Great Britain.

Crossing the elegant **O'Connell Bridge**, built in the 1790s, will take you over the River Liffey.

GRAFTON STREET & ST STEPHEN'S GREEN

Continuing south along Westmoreland Street, you will pass the imposing **Bank of Ireland** on your right and the grand entrance to **Trinity College** on your left *(see pp.31–2)*. Crossing Nassau Street will take you to pedestrianised **Grafton Street**. This area is home to Dublin's most upmarket shops and shopping arcades, like the **Powerscourt Centre** (59 South William Street; tel: 01-671 7000; Mon–Fri 10am–6pm, Thur until 8pm, Sat 9am–9pm).

Bewley's Oriental Café

About 100m/yds down Grafton Street, on your right, is **Bewley's Oriental Café**, see ⑪②. Dating from 1827, this Dublin institution is crammed full of teas, buns and Art Deco splendour. **Bewley's Café Theatre** (www.bewleys cafetheatre.com), with performances at 12.50pm every day except Sunday, is highly recommended. Short plays by the likes of Oscar Wilde, Sean O'Casey or new Irish writers, are performed as you tuck into a light lunch.

Shopping Street
Henry Street, to the west of O'Connell Street, is notable for its excellent shops, spearheaded by the revamped Arnott's department store.

Food & Drink 🍴

② **BEWLEY'S ORIENTAL CAFÉ**
78–9 Grafton Street; tel: 01-672 7720; http://bewleys.com; daily B, L and D; €–€€
This cavernous building contains a café bar and deli for breakfast, pastas and pizzas, plus a 'James Joyce' balcony and terrace, which is a favourite spot for afternoon tea (the scones are fabulous). Licensed.

Merrion Memorials

Merrion Square contains a sculpture of Oscar Wilde, reclining on a rock in the northwestern corner, and a jester's chair, dedicated to the late comic actor Dermot Morgan, star of the television series *Father Ted*.

St Stephen's Green

After lunch, a short stroll south down bustling Grafton Street takes you to leafy **St Stephen's Green** ❽. At the end of Grafton Street, cross over the road and through the Dublin Fusiliers Arch (1904) to enter the green, which was laid out in 1880. Walking around the green in an anti-clockwise direction, you will see statues of Irish patriot Robert Emmet; writers Yeats and Joyce; the Three Fates; and Wolfe Tone, leader of the 1798 Wexford Rebellion. Behind the monument is a memorial to those who died in the Great Famine of 1845–9.

On a sunny day, picnic provisions can be bought from the **Unicorn Food Emporium** on Merrion Row, see ⓘ⓷.

MERRION ROW & MERRION SQUARE

Leaving St Stephen's Green by the northeastern gate, turn right to find **Merrion Row**, packed full of trendy cafés and bistros, including **Hugo's** restaurant, see ⓘ⓸.

On the left-hand side is a surprising site: the tiny **Huguenot cemetery** ❾, built in 1693. Tucked in next to the imposing Sherbourne Hotel, the cemetery is usually locked, but you can peer through the railings to see the gravestones of the descendants of the Huguenots, French Protestants who had fled persecution in France. A list of the 239 surnames of those who are buried here can be seen on the wall

Below: door details, Merrion Square.

plaque to the left; this mentions the Becquett family, ancestors of the playwright Samuel Beckett.

Upper Merrion Street

At the end of Merrion Row, turn left onto Upper Merrion Street, home to **Restaurant Patrick Guilbaud**, see ⓘ⓹, Dublin's most exclusive restaurant. Continuing along Upper Merrion Street, you will see the imposing **Government Buildings** ❿, housing the office of the Prime Minister (Taoiseach), on your left (tel: 01-662 4888; www.heritageireland.ie; guided tours only, Sat 10.30am–1.30pm, every half hour; free; tickets can be collected on the morning of the tour from the National Gallery). Built in 1911 as the Royal College of Science, the Irish government occupied the northern wing in 1922. The Cabinet Room and the Ceremonial Staircase can be viewed on the tour.

The next building that you will see on your left is the **National Museum of Ireland – Natural History** (www.museum.ie; Tue–Sat 10am–5pm, Sun 2–5pm; free), built in 1856.

Merrion Square

Upper Merrion Street takes you straight to **Merrion Square** ⓫, the most famous of Dublin's Georgian squares, laid out between 1762 and 1764. If short of time, you can walk straight up Merrion Square West. However, it is worth taking the time to walk anti-clockwise around the streets that line the square.

Beginning at Merrion Square South, the houses progress in descending numerical order: look out for the old residences of W.B. Yeats (nos 82 and 52), the playwright Sheridan le Fanu (no. 70) and Daniel O'Connell (no. 52).

For a glimpse of what life was like in Georgian times you can visit **29 Lower Fitzwilliam Street ⓓ** at the southeastern corner of the square (tel: 01-7026 165; www.esb.ie/no29; Tue–Sat 10am–5pm, Sun noon–5pm; charge). The house has been restored with period furnishings that reflect the lifestyle of a middle-class family in the late 18th century.

Oscar Wilde House (closed to the public), on the northwestern corner at no. 1, was the first building to be built here. Wilde, born in 1855, lived here for the first 23 years of his life.

National Gallery of Ireland

Cross Merrion Square West into Clare Street. Here, on the left, is the entrance to the **National Gallery of Ireland ⓭** (Merrion Square West; tel: 01-661 5133; www.nationalgallery.ie; Mon–Sat 9.30am–5.30pm, Thur until 8.30pm, Sun noon–5.30pm; free). First opened in 1864, the gallery houses an enormous collection of Western European art ranging from the Middle Ages to the 20th century. It houses one of the most important collections of Irish art in the world, including the Yeats Museum (named after Jack B. Yeats) and the Millen-

nium Wing, dedicated to modern art.

For a well-earned drink, retrace your steps along Clare Street and turn left into the continuation of Merrion Square West. A right turn onto Fenian Street takes you to watering hole **The Ginger Man**, see ⑪⑥, popular with a young studenty crowd.

Food & Drink

③ **UNICORN CAFÉ, RESTAURANT AND FOOD EMPORIUM**
12b Merrion Court, Merrion Row; tel: 01-676 9755; Mon–Fri café 8am–8pm, restaurant 12.30–10.30pm; €–€€€
The Food Emporium offers exciting take-away food, such as gourmet sandwiches, 'designer' salads and smoothies. The café serves up good breakfasts, interesting lunches and early dinners. Meanwhile, the semi-formal restaurant, with an outdoor terrace, offers antipasti and Italian dishes.

④ **HUGO'S RESTAURANT AND WINE BAR**
6 Merrion Row; tel: 01-676 5955; daily noon–11pm; €€–€€€
An award-winning bar and restaurant, Hugo's offers modern European and fusion cuisine – such as crispy duck confit, seared scallops and wild venison – with an emphasis on locally sourced and organic produce. For a less pricey option, try their pre-theatre or 'Afternoon Bites' menus.

⑤ **RESTAURANT PATRICK GUILBAUD**
21 Upper Merrion Street; tel 01-676 4192; www.restaurant patrickguilbaud.ie; Tue–Sat L and D; €€€€
With two Michelin stars and a reputation for using the finest seasonal ingredients, this is contemporary French cooking at its best. Avoid bankruptcy with the good-value set lunch.

⑥ **THE GINGER MAN**
40 Fenian Street; tel: 01-676 6388; daily, until 2.30am at weekends; €–€€
This traditional Irish pub, set over three floors and with an outdoor terrace, is tucked away behind the Davenport Hotel. There is a good range of beers on tap, the wine is moderately priced, and it serves Irish pub-grub.

WICKLOW

Wicklow, just south of Dublin, is a county of contrasts, where desolate mountaintop roads give way to plunging river valleys. This drive takes in the spectacular scenery of the Great Sugar Loaf Mountain and the Sally Gap, descends into ethereal Glendalough and finishes at the sleepy village of Avoca.

DISTANCE 75km (47 miles)
TIME A full day
START Enniskerry
END Avoca (or Arklow)
POINTS TO NOTE

Enniskerry is on the R117, 6km (4 miles) south of junction 14 of the M50. If driving from Dublin, the R117 starts south of St Stephen's Green, on Charlemont Street. To return to Dublin at the end of the drive, take the R747 from Avoca to Arklow, and then the N11 north. Alternatively, to get to Kilkenny (tour 4), travel west on the R747 and R727 to Carlow, and join the N9 and N10 southwest to Kilkenny.

As this is a scenic mountain route, with an hour or so between some of the stops, it is worth taking provisions with you. Several points in the drive, such as Glencree and Glendalough, offer excellent walking.

Wicklow Way

The Wicklow Way, one of Ireland's great long-distance walking routes, extends 132km (82 miles) southwest from Marlay Park, just south of Dublin, to Clonegal in County Carlow. You can pick it up a few kilometres past Powerscourt, to the west of Killough.

This drive showcases both the spectacular greenery that has earned Wicklow the title 'garden of Ireland' and the rugged charms of the granite Wicklow Mountains. It also takes in the Georgian grandeur of the Powerscourt Estate and the mystical delights of Glendalough, one of the oldest monastic settlements in Ireland.

ENNISKERRY & POWERSCOURT

Begin the tour at **Enniskerry ❶**, a quiet country town built into a hillside, where you can buy provisions for the day and have morning coffee and cake at the delightful **Kingfisher's Kitchen**, see ⑪①, overlooking the town square (note that there is a free car park off the R117, to the west of the square).

Powerscourt Estate & Waterfall
Enniskerry is dominated by the enormous **Powerscourt Estate ❷** (tel: 01-204 6000; www.powerscourt.ie; daily 9.30am–5.30pm, until dusk in winter; charge), just south of the town. To get there, follow the main road uphill, passing the town square on your right; Powerscourt is clearly signposted off the road. Although the estate dates back to 1300, when the Le Poer family – later anglicised to

Power – built a castle here, the Palladian-style mansion and landscaped gardens that you see today were completed in the late 18th century and were restored, following a fire, in the mid-1990s. A visit to the estate gives an insight into the lifestyle of the super-rich Anglo-Irish during the Romantic period.

There is a separate entrance (and entry charge) for the stunning **Powerscourt Waterfall** ❸ (daily Mar–Oct 10.30am–5.30pm, Nov–Feb 10.30am–4pm, May–Aug 9.30am–7pm), the highest in Ireland at 121m (398ft). To reach it, leave the mansion and gardens and turn right uphill; the road twists and turns for several kilometres.

WICKLOW MOUNTAIN DRIVE

Glencree and Sugar Loaf Mountain
Heading back towards the estate, turn left and take the road that skirts the river valley. After about 15 minutes, the road meets the R115. A right turn will take you to the small village of **Glencree** ❹, set into the Glencree valley, with its unusual Peace and Reconciliation Centre (founded in 1974 during 'The Troubles'), former British army barracks and café (see www.glencree.ie).

Glencree affords stunning views, looking east, of the **Great Sugar Loaf Mountain**, Wicklow's highest point at 503m (1,650ft).

Above from far left: Powerscourt Waterfall; entrance hall to the estate.

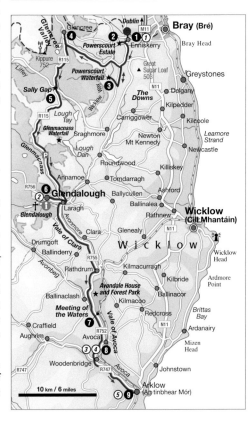

Sally Gap

Leaving Glencree, return to the R115 and follow the road south towards the **Sally Gap ⑤**. This desolate, barren mountain pass is surprisingly flat, allowing for astonishing views of the steely Wicklow mountains. There is a parking spot 10km (6 miles) further on at **Glenmacnass**, where you can visit a gorgeous waterfall.

Trials of St Kevin

Legend has it that St Kevin, a handsome but chaste monk, had to fend off some amorous suitors. In one case, he threw himself naked into a patch of nettles and his suitor into an icy lake, to spurn her advances (and, presumably, his impure thoughts).

Right: Glendalough, monastery gatehouse.

Avondale House

Just outside Rathdrum, on the L2149, are Avondale House and Forest Park (tel: 0404-46111; house: noon–4pm Jul–Aug daily, June and Sept Tue–Sun, Apr–May and Oct weekends only, by appointment rest of year; park: daily 8.30am–7.30pm; charge), the birthplace and home of national hero and later disgraced politician Charles Stewart Parnell *(see also p.35)*. The house, built by James Wyatt in 1779 and surrounded by 202ha (500 acres) of tree trails and walks, was recently restored according to its 1850 decor.

GLENDALOUGH TO AVOCA

The road descends to arrive, after another 10–15 minutes, at the river valley of **Glendalough ⑥**. At the end of the R115, take a right along the R756 to reach the free Visitor Centre car park (there is a charge for the higher car park). The **Visitor Centre** itself (tel: 0404-45352/45325; mid-Oct–mid-Mar 9.30am–5pm, mid-Mar–mid-Apr 9.30am–6pm) charges admission.

The name Glendalough derives from Irish Gaelic 'Gleann dá Locha', meaning 'Glen of the two Lakes'; the upper lake, a short walk along the river valley, is much the bigger of the two. St Kevin first established a monastic settlement in 498AD, and monks continued to study and live here until the 1600s. The upper lake has the better scenery and the original sites of St Kevin's settlement and habitations. The lower lake contains many impressive architectural sights, including the monastery gatehouse (the only surviving example of its kind in the country), the 10th-century St Mary's Church and tiny round tower, and a 12th-century Priest's House.

Leaving Glendalough, a good option for lunch is the **Wicklow Heather Restaurant**, see ⑪②.

Vale of Clara

Head back along the R756, following the signs to Avoca. After a few kilometres turn right onto the R755 and continue southeast, driving parallel to

the Avonmore River. The road descends into the gently wooded **Vale of Clara**, passing through the small village of **Rathdrum**. Nearby are **Avondale House and Forest Park** *(see feature, left)*.

Meeting of the Waters

Some 8km (5 miles) past Rathdrum (taking the R752 south) is the **Meeting of the Waters ❼**, the point at which the rivers Avonbeg and Avonmore converge to form the River Avoca. Set deep in the Vale of Avoca, this is a surprisingly moody place, blanketed by trees. Thomas Moore gave the spot its name in an 1808 poem, which is inscribed on a wall.

Avoca

A few minutes further on, set just off the main road alongside the river, is delightful **Avoca ❽**. Although it still trades on its fame as location for the 1990s BBC series *Ballykissangel*, the main draw of the village is **Avoca Handweavers** (Old Mill, Main Street; tel: 0402-35105; www.avoca.ie; summer 9am–6pm, winter 9.30am–5.30pm). The weavers here have been producing linens from Ireland's oldest working mill since 1723; you can see them in action in the weaving sheds. The fruits of their labours – including rugs and bed linen, clothing and accessories – are sold here in the mill shop, and in stores throughout Ireland. The mill also has an excellent **café**, see ⓘ③.

If you wish to eat something more substantial, **Hendley's**, opposite Fitzgerald's pub, is a good option, see ⓘ④.

Arklow

Alternatively, you can continue southeast from Avoca along the R747 to **Arklow ❾**, Wicklow's busiest town and once a thriving port, to dine at local favourite **Kitty's of Arklow**, see ⓘ⑤.

Above from far left: Powerscourt garden and the Great Sugar Loaf Mountain beyond; blankets at Avoca Handweavers; Glendalough lower lake scenery.

Food & Drink

② WICKLOW HEATHER RESTAURANT
R756 just before Glendalough (south side of road); tel: 0404-45157; daily L and D; €–€€
A pub/restaurant on the tourist trail with prices to match. The menu is better value at lunch, when you can get a goat's cheese open sandwich or a crispy chicken salad, as well as mains and specials. There's a pleasant outdoor terrace.

③ AVOCA HANDWEAVERS CAFÉ AND PANTRY
The Mill at Avoca Village; tel: 0402-35105; daily 9.30am–5.30pm (winter until 5pm); €
Inside the Avoca Handweavers is a retro-style pantry and deli, selling delicious tea, cakes (scones, rock cakes and buns), soup and sandwiches.

④ HENDLEY'S FISH AND CHIP RESTAURANT AND TAKE-AWAY
Avoca Village; tel: 0402-30937; Wed–Sun noon–10pm; €
More than your average fish-and-chip restaurant, Hendley's serves the 'daily catch' as well as smoked fish specials at very reasonable prices. Situated right next to the river.

⑤ KITTY'S OF ARKLOW
Main Street, Arklow; tel: 0402-31669; noon–5pm and 6–10.30pm; €€–€€€
The most popular restaurant in town, Kitty's has a lounge bar and a more expensive upstairs restaurant with harbour views. Fresh fish specials – scallops, mussels, seafood chowder – sit beside traditional dishes, such as Wicklow lamb or steak. Set menus are available at lunchtime and for 'early bird' diners.

KILKENNY

Explore Kilkenny's castle and medieval centre before driving through pictur-esque villages on the River Nore to tranquil Jerpoint Abbey deep in the countryside. Finish off aboard a famine ship at New Ross in County Wexford.

DISTANCE City walk: 2km (1¼ miles); drive: 46km (28½ miles)
TIME A 2-hour city walk followed by a half-day drive
START Kilkenny city
END New Ross
POINTS TO NOTE
Kilkenny is 116km (72 miles) south-west of Dublin and approximately 100km (62 miles) west of Arklow. New Ross is 14km (8 miles) north-east of Waterford, starting point of tour 5, and 53km (33 miles) west of Rosslare ferryport.

Cobbled Alleys

At first sight Kilkenny's main street appears to be a typical town high street. But note the narrow covered passageways on either side that lead to cobbled alleyways lined by small houses. Known as 'slips', these are a particular feature of Kilkenny. Some are now lined by modern housing, but all are well cared for, with floral displays in summer.

KILKENNY CITY

Kilkenny ❶ was founded by St Canice in the 6th century; in its 14th-century prime, it was the venue for many English parliaments, rivalling Dublin in importance. Its compact centre has several medieval buildings, but the star of the show is Kilkenny Castle, set in rich parklands beside the River Nore.

Kilkenny Castle

Follow signs for the city centre which will lead you to **Kilkenny Castle ❹** (tel: 056-772 1450; www.heritageireland.ie; daily 9.30am–5.30pm, Oct–Mar until 4.30pm; charge, gardens free), an unmistakable landmark beside a large public car park. The original castle was built in the 13th century, but the present building dates mainly from 1820. Inside its huge entrance gate you are greeted by a magnificent panorama in which the mature trees of the castle's parklands frame the distant countryside, with a formal rose garden and fountain in the foreground. The seat of the Butler family (the Dukes of Ormond), two wings of the castle have been restored in the style of a grand country house circa 1830. They contain a library, drawing room and long gallery.

Kilkenny Design Craft Centre

Cross the road in front of the castle to visit its stable block, an elegant semi-circular construction in the classical style, topped by a copper dome and weather vane. It now houses the **Kilkenny Design Craft Centre ❸** (tel: 056-772 2118; www.kilkenny design.com; Mon–Sat 10am–7pm, Sun 11am–7pm; free), one of Ireland's best craft shops. Also here is the headquarters of the Crafts Council of Ireland, which has exhibitions of

contemporary craft work (free), and a **restaurant**, see ①. There are also several small craft studios and factory outlets. A gate at the rear leads to the pleasant gardens of **Butler House**, the castle's dower house.

Medieval Town Centre

Turn left out of the Design Centre, past some fine 18th-century houses, and turn right at the traffic lights onto Rose Inn Street. **Shee Alms House** ❻, a stone building constructed in 1594 to house the poor, is now the **Tourist Information Office** (tel: 056-775 1500; www.kilkennytourism.ie). Go up to the first floor, and exit onto a narrow alleyway, turning left. This leads to the High Street *(see margin, left)*.

Turn right and walk past the **Tholsel** ❺, Kilkenny's former toll-house, which was built in 1761 and has an arcade over the pavement and an octagonal clock tower. Beyond this, on the opposite side of the road, is **Rothe House and Garden** ❺ (Parliament Street; tel: 056-772 2893; www.rothehouse.com; Apr–Oct Mon–Sat 10.30am–5pm, Sun 3–6pm, Nov–Mar Mon–Sat 10.30am–5pm, Sun 2–6pm; charge), a 16th-century merchant's fortified home, which now houses a museum of local history.

St Canice's Cathedral

From Rothe House, on your left you can see **St Canice's Cathedral** ❺ (tel: 056-776 4971; Mon–Sat 10am–1pm, Sun 2–5pm; charge), named after the

city's founder, on a height above the town. It is approached from Parliament Street up a flight of stone steps and under an arch. The cathedral, with its massive round tower and stepped battlements, dates from the 13th cen-

Above from far left: Kilkenny Castle; a city tea room; potter at work in the Design Craft Centre.

Food & Drink

① **KILKENNY DESIGN CRAFT CENTRE**
Castle Yard, Kilkenny; tel: 056-772 2118; www.kilkenny design.com; daily 10am–7pm, Jan–Mar closed Sun; €
This lively first-floor self-service restaurant is popular with locals and visitors. All food is freshly prepared, using local ingredients where possible. Wholesome daily specials, like chicken and broccoli crumble with Lavistown cheese, feature alongside imaginative soups, salads and home-baked cakes.

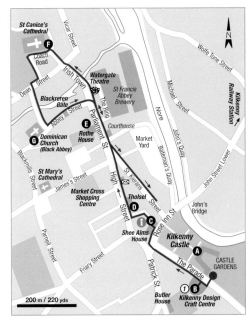

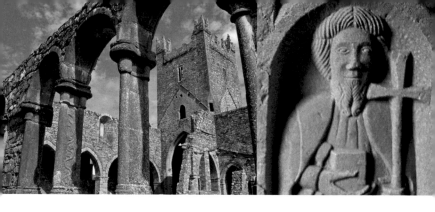

Wexford

County Wexford borders Wicklow to the north, Kilkenny to the west and Waterford to the south. Its long coastline to the east has many sandy beaches. If you are arriving by car at Rosslare, Wexford town, 18km (11 miles) northwest of the ferryport, makes a pleasant stop. Small and easy to explore on foot, it consists of a series of quays parallel to the water and a main street one block inland, with small, old-fashioned shops and pubs. At Ferrycarrig, 5km (3 miles) northwest of Wexford town on the N11, is the Irish National Heritage Park (tel: 053-20733; www.inhp.com; charge). This open-air museum on the banks of the River Slaney provides a useful introduction to Ireland's history and architecture from Stone Age man (6,000BC) to the arrival of the Normans in the 12th century. New Ross is 37km (23 miles) west of Wexford on the N25.

tury, and is believed to be on the site of St Canice's monastic foundation. Oliver Cromwell's soldiers left it a roofless ruin, and it has been much restored over the years, but it still has some fine medieval monuments. Wooden steps inside the 30m (98ft) tall **round tower** (charge) can be climbed in the summer months.

Black Abbey

Leave the cathedral by the main gate leading to Dean Street. Cross over and follow the finger signpost down an alley that crosses a canal to the **Dominican Church**. It incorporates the slender

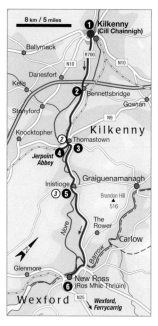

tower and 14th-century windows of the **Black Abbey ⑥**, dating from 1225; in the forecourt is an unusual collection of mid-13th-century stone coffins.

Turn left out of the church and follow the 'slip' back to Parliament Street. Turn right, and at the fork take the lower street, St Kieran's, a lively pedstrianised area, once the heart of the medieval town; it leads back to Rose Inn Street and the castle.

NORE VALLEY

Head straight out of town from the castle and join the R700, a pretty minor road that follows the River Nore southwards to its estuary.

Bennettsbridge

The stone bridge at **Bennettsbridge ❷**, 6km (3¾ miles) south of Kilkenny, dates from 1285 and is one of the oldest crossings of the River Nore. The road swings right over the bridge, and passes **Chesneau Leather Goods**, (056-772 7456; www.chesneaudesign.com) a factory outlet selling fine leather handbags, which marks the start of the **Kilkenny Craft Trail** *(see margin, right)*.

Thomastown & Jerpoint Abbey

Thomastown ❸, 12km (7 miles) further south, is an attractive village of grey-stone buildings and steep hills that dates from the 13th century. You could stop for lunch here at the **Watergarden Café**, see ⑪②.

Follow the signs in the village for a 2km (1 mile) detour southwest across another narrow stone bridge to **Jerpoint Abbey ④** (tel: 056-772 4623; www.heritageireland.ie; daily Mar–Oct 9am–5pm, Nov–early Dec 9.30am–4pm; charge). Founded in 1158 by the Cistercians, this is one of the finest monastic ruins in Ireland, consisting of a cloister, quadrangle and three-naved church with Romanesque arches set against a peaceful rural backdrop. Walk around the two sides of the cloisters to appreciate their unusual carvings, some of which are like medieval cartoons.

Inistioge

Return to Thomastown and rejoin the R700 south, crossing the Nore again via a long, 12-arched stone bridge, amid sweeping views of a wooded valley, the location of **Inistioge ⑤**. The village is situated on a bend of the river and has a tree-lined square leading to a tall stone bridge. It's a favourite location for films, which include *Widow's Peak* (1994) with Mia Farrow and Joan Plowright, and *Circle of Friends* (1995) with Minnie Driver and Saffron Burrows. Follow the road to the left at the Woodstock Arms for the riverfront. A flat grassy area next to the river is a perfect spot for picnicking, with a view of the picturesque bridge backed by a line of Georgian houses. One of these is a restaurant, **Footlights**, see ⑪③.

NEW ROSS

Continue along the R700 for another 17km (10½ miles), crossing the border into County Wexford *(see margin, left)* at **New Ross ⑥**. The town was built on a steep hill overlooking the River Barrow at a strategically important river crossing. On the river bank you will see the tall masts of the ***Dunbrody* Famine Ship** (tel: 051-425239; www.dunbrody.com; tours daily 9am–6pm, Oct–Mar until 5pm; charge), a full-scale replica of a sailing ship built in 1845 to transport emigrants to North America. On board, actors tell the stories of the passengers, who travelled in appalling conditions in this 'coffin-ship' in order to escape the Great Famine. It is both entertaining and a sobering reminder of the ordeal suffered by the 2 million plus people who emigrated from this port.

Above from far left:
Jerpoint Abbey
view and detail; St
Canice's Cathedral in
Kilkenny; Inistioge.

Kilkenny Craft Trail
Pick up a leaflet at the Kilkenny Design Craft Centre, the Kilkenny Tourist Office or Chesneau Leather Goods (see also www.kilkennytourism.ie) for details of all the outlets participating in the Crafts Trail. Based in Kilkenny, Bennettsbridge, Jerpoint, Thomastown and Stoneyford, they include makers of ceramics, jewellery, hand-blown glass and wooden furniture.

Food & Drink 🍴

② WATERGARDEN CAFÉ
Ladywell Street, Thomastown; tel: 056-772 4690; Mon–Fri 10am–4.30pm; €
This simple café, beside a garden centre and craft shop, backs onto a delightful stream-side garden overhung by weeping willows. Enjoy a delicious light lunch of home-made soup, home-grown salad and freshly baked desserts.

③ FOOTLIGHTS
The Square, Inistioge; tel: 086-361 9411; www.footlights.ie; daily noon–8pm, Fri–Sat until 10pm, Nov–Mar Sat and Sun only; €€
The decor is stylishly contemporary at this child-friendly bistro in a period riverside house. Snacks include ciabattas, salads and pizzas, while mains are made with fresh local produce.

WATERFORD &
THE ROCK OF CASHEL

Explore Waterford city's 18th-century quayside then drive to the iconic Rock of Cashel. Cross the scenic Vee Gap through the Knockmealdown Mountains then potter around pretty Lismore village, dominated by a grey-stone castle.

DISTANCE 122km (76 miles)

TIME A full day

START Waterford city

END Lismore

POINTS TO NOTE

On Sundays, most sights and shops in Waterford city will be closed. From Waterford to Cashel via Clonmel is 71km (44 miles). If you are driving to the southwest from Dublin, start the tour at Cashel. From Cashel to Lismore is 51km (32 miles). From Lismore you can return to Waterford (63km/39 miles) on the N72 and N25 or continue west on the N72 to Fermoy and N8 to Cork (49.5km/30 miles).

Food & Drink

① THE GRANARY

Merchant's Quay, tel: 051-304500; B, L and AT; €

The self-service counter is packed with home-baked treats like lemon meringue pie or foccacia. There's a sheltered outdoor patio, and sofas and tables in the museum lobby.

Waterford is the largest city in the southeast, but even then it only has a population of about 50,000. Founded by the Vikings in 853, it was the first settlement to be occupied by the Normans, who came from Wales in 1170. It owes its historic importance to its sheltered location on the mouth of the River Suir, and its proximity to the Welsh coast.

The rural counties of Waterford and Tipperary have rich fertile plains and small, quiet towns. The mighty Rock of Cashel, once home to the Kings of Munster, is a legacy of the area's wealth and strategic importance in pre-Christian and medieval times.

WATERFORD CITY

In its 18th-century heyday **Waterford ❶** was an important port, and its long quays, though awaiting redevelopment, are still impressive. Quaint, cobbled streets alternate with gracefully proportioned Georgian buildings. The building of the largely pedestrianised shopping centre unearthed many treasures from its Viking and Norman past, now displayed in a fine museum.

The Quays

Park on the quays, and if the weather is fine, stroll up towards the town clock along the once busy cut-stone docks. Then head for the unmistakable pepper-pot bastion **Reginald's Tower** (tel: 051-304500; www.heritageireland. ie; daily 10am–5pm, to 6pm June– mid-Sept, mid-Sept–Mar Wed–Sun only; charge) at the quays' eastern extremity. This 12th-century drum tower is 24m (80ft) tall and has been used as a mint, prison and military store *(see margin, right)*. It is now restored and houses a collection of treasures that includes Viking and Norman artefacts unearthed in recent excavations. Highlights include a gold brooch from 1210AD, a sword given by Henry VIII to Waterford's Mayor in 1536, and 18th-century Irish silver.

The ground floor is home to one of the town's most popular daytime eating spots, **The Granary**, see ①①.

Waterford Crystal Visitor Centre

Turn right out of Reginald's Tower and walk inland along the Mall to the new headquarters of **Waterford Crystal** (tel: 051-317000; www.waterfordvisitor centre.com; factory tours Nov–Mar Mon–Sat 9am–3.15pm, Apr–Oct until 4.15pm, Sun 9.30am–4.15pm; charge). 'Old Waterford Glass', a heavy lead crystal produced between 1783 and 1851, is much sought-after by collectors for its outstanding light-refracting properties. Following bankruptcy in 2009, Waterford Crystal is again being produced in the city, and the dramatic factory tour is as popular as ever. Book in advance online to avoid queuing.

Conquerors
Ireland was never conquered by the Romans, and the introduction of Christianity in the 5th century was a peaceful process. The first hostile invaders were the Vikings in the 9th century, while the Normans, who landed at Waterford from Wales in 1169, inter-married with Irish nobles and were quickly assimilated. Strongbow, a Norman conqueror, married Aoife (or Eve), daughter of the Irish chief Dermot Mac-Murrough, at Reginald's Tower in 1170.

ROCK OF CASHEL

Leave Waterford on the N24 , heading west through **Carrick-on-Suir** and **Clonmel ❷**. The latter is a busy market town on the River Suir known for its apple orchards and cider-making. About 500m/yds west of Clonmel, take the R688 northwest to Cashel.

The **Rock of Cashel ❸** (tel: 062-61437; www.heritageireland.ie; daily 9am–5.30pm, June–mid-Sept until 7pm, mid-Oct–mid-Mar until 4.30pm; charge), a 63m (206ft) limestone outcrop topped with ruined towers and gables, looms up suddenly from the flat plain. Its unexpected beauty causes a sharp intake of breath.

The Rock was originally a stronghold of the Kings of Munster who ruled southwest Ireland during the early Middle Ages. On converting to Christianity in 1101, King Muirchertach Ua Briain gave his fortress to the Church. Most of the buildings here date from the 13th to 15th centuries.

Exploring the Rock

After buying your ticket, turn right into the enclosure to avoid following the herd, then stroll around the northern perimeter, enjoying views of the plains of Tipperary. Note the high-up entrance at the base of the round tower, which made it a safe refuge.

Now walk through the roofless Gothic cathedral to the **Crossing**, a complex arch where two churches interlink. Turn left out of the cathedral to **Cormac's Chapel**, one of Europe's finest examples of Hiberno-Romanesque architecture. Look up at the huge rounded arches above each of the doors, and the ingenious curved roof.

Cashel Town

It is only a few minutes' walk south, past an old chapel now converted into a fine-dining restaurant, **Chez Hans**, and an adjacent daytime **café**, see ⑪②, to the centre of **Cashel**, a quiet country town with some old-fashioned wooden shop fronts. Turn south for the **Heritage Centre** (Main Street; tel: 062-62511; www.cashel.ie; daily 9.30am–5.30pm; free), which has a display about the historical relationship between the town and the Rock, and a scale model of Cashel in the 1600s; it also contains the Tourist Information Office.

VEE GAP

Drive south on the N8, taking the R670 for **Cahir ❹** and following it as it turns sharply right down a hill through the town. Cahir's most notable feature is its **castle** (tel: 052-744 1011; www.heritage ireland.ie; daily 9.30am–5.30pm, mid-Oct–mid-Mar until 4.30pm; charge), a massive 12th-century limestone fortress set on a rock in the River Suir.

The R668 to Clogheen is on the left immediately after the castle. As you drive towards Ballylooby, the **Knockmealdown Mountains** are straight

Below: aspects of Lismore Castle.

ahead. Take a sharp left in **Clogheen** for the **Vee Gap** ❺, a scenic mountain pass. The road curves around a peat-covered mountain, past a black corrie lake, to a height of 653m (2,144ft). Park here and look back across the flat plain of Tipperary to Cahir at the foot of the Galtee Mountains. Up here, there are no inhabitants (just sheep) and the vegetation is mainly grass and heather. Descending into the valley of the Blackwater River, the vegetation increases, with rhododendrons and a rich undergrowth of ferns.

LISMORE

Continue south on the R688. As you cross the bridge into **Lismore** ❻ you will have a dramatic view of **Lismore Castle**, perched on a cliff above the River Blackwater. This mid-19th-century building is the Irish residence of the Duke of Devonshire; it is not open to the public. The village itself was home to a 6th-century monastery founded by St Carthage and was built to house the workers on the Duke's estates; during the famine years the people of Lismore suffered particularly badly.

Park and walk to the **Lismore Heritage Centre** (058-54975; www.discover lismore.com; Mon–Fri 9am–5.30pm, May–Oct also Sat 10am–5.30pm and Sun noon–5.30pm; charge). Formerly the town courthouse, the centre has a shop, tourist information, and a video presentation on the town's history.

Village Walk

Turn right and walk along Lismore's main street. Among the pleasant mix of shops and antiques stores are several pubs and restaurants, including **O'Brien Chop House**, see ③. Turn left up the broad North Mall, which leads to **St Carthage's Cathedral** (daily 9.30am–5.30pm; free), a modest mid-17th-century church in the neo-Gothic style with some interesting memorial stones from an earlier 9th-century church. Take the cobbled footpath to the left of the church leading downhill, and turn left at the main road to return to the car park.

Just here is the entrance to **Lismore Castle Gardens and Art Gallery** (tel: 058-54424; www.lismorecastle.com; daily Apr, May and Sept 1.45–4.45pm, June–Aug 11am–4.45pm; charge). The (3ha) 7 acres of gardens consist of woodland walks and contemporary sculpture, with good views of the castle.

Above from far left: Rock of Cashel; rhododendrons in the valley of the Blackwater River.

Food & Drink

② CAFÉ HANS

Moor Lane, Cashel; tel: 062-63660; Tue–Sun L; €

This great café occupies a tiny chapel-like building below the Rock. The small menu offers salads, open sandwiches and a couple of daily specials featuring local produce, such as Tipperary lamb and Rossmore mussels.

③ O'BRIEN CHOP HOUSE

Main Street, Lismore; tel: 058-53810; Wed–Sat L & D, Sun L; daily July and Aug; €–€€

The O'Brien pub, now transformed into a restaurant that retains the character and charm of the Victorian original. Locally sourced meat and veg traditionally prepared in hearty servings, and home baking all year round.

CORK CITY & HARBOUR

After a walking tour of the centre of Cork city, including its bustling indoor food market and renowned art gallery, visit a thriving wildlife park, a classic shooting lodge surrounded by gardens and Cobh, formerly Queenstown, departure point for most of Ireland's 19th- and 20th-century emigrants.

Above: summer fruits at the English Market.

Up & Down

The northern side of the city rises steeply from the river and wits like to joke that this is the origin of the distinctly 'up and down' Cork accent. You will hear fine examples of this on St Patrick Street in the afternoons, when newspaper sellers hawk the *Evening Echo* with loud cries of 'Eeeeeko'.

DISTANCE City walk: 0.75km (½ mile); driving tour: 24.5km (15 miles)
TIME 1 or 2 days
START Cork city
END Cobh
POINTS TO NOTE

Allow two days if you include a visit to the university. Note that Cork is busiest on Saturdays and quietest on Mondays. Most city attractions are closed on Sundays.

Trains run to Fota and Cobh every half hour from Kent Station (Lower Glanmire Road; 021-450 6766; www.irishrail.ie), on the city's northern side.

From Cork, you can head 30km (18 miles) south to Kinsale (tour 7), or west on the N22 to Killarney and the Ring of Kerry (tour 8) and Tralee and the Dingle Peninsula (tour 9).

Cork's city centre is built on an island formed by two channels of the River Lee. In the 18th and early 19th century cargoes of butter, beef and animal hides were exported from the city's many quays, creating a rich merchant class who built an attractive city of bridges and steeples. In the 19th century shipping moved downstream to the deep-water harbour at Cobh. The view of Cobh's steeply terraced houses beneath the soaring Gothic cathedral was the last, often tear-blurred, sight most emigrants had of their homeland.

CORK CITY

Start at the **Tourist Information Office** (tel: 021-425 5100; www.cometo cork.ie) on **Grand Parade ①**. Directly across the road note the terrace of three elegant Georgian houses with slate-hung, bow-fronted windows, remnants of Cork's 18th-century prime.

English Market

Turn right for the **English Market ②** (Mon–Sat 9am–5.30pm), a Victorian covered market. Step back to view the imposing classical entrance. (It's worth looking up regularly in Cork to enjoy the ornate Victorian facades that often survive above the modern shop fronts.) A foodie-heaven, the market has about 150 stalls, from traditional butchers to

purveyors of farmhouse cheeses and hand-made chocolates; do not miss the alley of freshly landed seafood. Walking straight through the market will bring you to a piazza where **Farmgate Café** occupies an overhead balcony, see ①①.

St Patrick & Paul Streets
Turn left from the market into Princes' Street and then right onto **St Patrick Street ❸**, a wide curved thoroughfare and the traditional place for a Saturday afternoon promenade. Cross the street and follow the pedestrian alley to **Paul Street ❹**. This is Cork's 'left bank', with antiques shops, bookshops, art galleries, boutiques, cafés and buskers.

Crawford Municipal Art Gallery
At the northeastern end of Paul Street, the **Crawford Municipal Art Gallery ❺** (Emmett Place; tel: 021-480 5042; www.crawfordartgallery.ie; Mon–Sat 10am–5pm, Thur until 9pm; free) is a large, Dutch-style red-brick building that dates from 1724; it was originally Cork's Custom House. The collection is strong on 18th–21st-century British and Irish painting, stained glass and classical sculpture. The **Crawford Gallery Café**, see ①②, is a favourite meeting spot with excellent fresh food.

Turn left from the gallery and walk past the 1965 **Cork Opera House** *(see p.122)* along a wide piazza. This leads to the River Lee, with the steep northern side of Cork city opposite *(see margin, left)*. Turn right (east) for

St Patrick's Bridge ❻, the northern extremity of Patrick Street, which you can follow back to Grand Parade.

Above from far left: English Market; bridge to Grand Parade.

Food & Drink

① **FARMGATE CAFÉ**
English Market, Princes Street; tel: 021-427 8134; Mon–Sat, L and AT; €
A unique venue on a terrace above the English Market's bustle. All food is sourced in the market; choose from home-made soups, quiches and imaginative open sandwiches or the more substantial table-service menu, including shepherd's pie and the catch of the day.

② **CRAWFORD GALLERY CAFÉ**
Emmet Place; tel: 021-427 4415; B. L and AT (to 4pm); €
This elegant room with tall windows is a restful haven. A team from Ballymaloe, Ireland's famous country house, offer light seasonal specials and legendary home-made cakes.

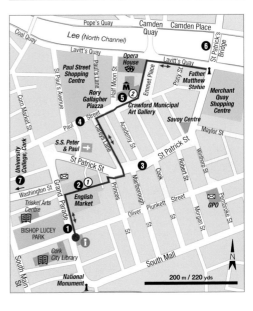

Above from left: giraffes at Fota Wildlife Park; colourful Cobh houses.

University College

To extend your city tour, hop on a no. 8 bus outside Debenham's department store on St Patrick Street to **University College Cork** ❼ (Western Road; tel: 021-490 1876; www.ucc.ie;

visitor centre Mon–Fri 9am–5pm; free), with some 15,000 students. Highlights here include the Tudor-Gothic-style quadrangle (1854), the Crawford Observatory (1878), the Hiberno-Romanesque-style Honan Chapel (1916), the Glucksman Gallery (2005), displaying contemporary art, and a superb collection of Ogham stones inscribed with the Celtic alphabet.

CORK HARBOUR

You can travel to Fota and Cobh either by rail or road. Note that the 25-minute train ride from Kent Station *(see box, p.52)* provides dramatic sea views that cannot be seen from a car. If you are driving, you should follow the N8 then the N22 east, turning off at the Fota and Cobh signpost after 10km (6 miles).

Fota Island

Fota Island ❽ and Cobh are both on the shores of Cork's outer harbour. The 47ha (116 acre) estate of Fota House is surrounded by several kilometres of stone wall, and contains a golf course and luxury hotel. Go to the second entrance for **Fota Wildlife Park** (tel: 021-481 2678; www.fotawildlife.ie; Mon–Sat 10am–6pm, Sun 11am–6pm; charge), which has giraffes, wallabies, ostriches, zebras and antelopes roaming free, plus a large enclosure for cheetahs. The car park (charge) also serves **Fota House, Gardens and Arboretum** (tel: 021-481 5543; www.fotahouse.com;

Kiss the Blarney

Blarney Castle (tel: 021-438 5252; www.blarneycastle.ie; daily 9am–sundown, Sun until 5.30pm in summer; charge), 10km (6 miles) northwest of Cork city, is still a must for first-time visitors. The building itself (one of Ireland's biggest tower houses) is impressive in bulk, although it is a roofless ruin, and you must climb a spiral of 84 stone steps (wear trainers) to reach the top. To kiss the famous Blarney Stone – in the hope of acquiring 'the gift of the gab' – you need to lie on your back and lean your head out over the castle's ramparts while being held securely by staff who handle some 300,000 stone-kissers a year. The 15th-century castle is situated in a landscaped park with a large lake and two rivers, and is surrounded by 'Druidic' rock gardens. The whole experience is presented tongue-in-cheek as a load of Blarney, but nevertheless makes a good half-day outing. Across the village green at Ireland's biggest craft shop, Blarney Woollen Mills (021-451 6111; www.blarney.com), you can acquire a sweater and a woolly hat to complete your Irish initiation.

gardens: daily 9am–6pm, free; house: Apr–Oct Mon–Sat 10am–5pm, Sun 11am–5pm, last entry 4pm, Nov–Mar phone ahead; charge). The arboretum is over 200 years old and includes rhododendrons and azaleas (at their best in late spring). The Regency-style house was originally a shooting lodge; its servants' quarters retain many original features and there are impressive plaster ceilings in the ground-floor rooms.

Cobh

The road from Fota to **Cobh** ❾ (pronounced 'cove') skirts the edge of Cork Harbour for 6km (3¾ miles). About 1km (½ mile) beyond the cranes of an abandoned dockyard, look out for a signpost on the right to **Cobh Heritage Centre** (tel: 021-481 3591; www. cobhheritage.com; Mon–Sat 9.30am–6pm, Sun 9.30am–6pm; free) and park beside it. If you are coming by train, the station is next to the Heritage Centre.

The Centre occupies a Victorian railway station beside a deep-water berth once used by transatlantic liners. Cobh

was the last port of call for the 'unsinkable' RMS *Titanic* in 1912 and also received survivors and the drowned from RMS *Lusitania*, sunk off the coast by a German submarine in 1915. At the time, the town was called Queenstown, having been renamed to celebrate the visit of Queen Victoria in 1849 (it reverted to Cobh in 1920). Within the Centre, **The Queenstown Story** (tel: 021-481 3591; www.cobhheritage.com; daily 9.30am–5pm; charge) is a lively audiovisual display about the town's seafaring past and Irish emigration.

From here, walk towards the town, an attractive south-facing Victorian resort, past the **Jacob's Ladder** restaurant, see , with a great sea view.

The seafront has a Victorian town park and opposite is the ***Lusitania Memorial***, dedicated to the 1,198 people who died when the ocean liner sank on 7 May 1915. Overhead is the tall spire of the neo-Gothic **St Colman's Cathedral**. Walk up to its entrance for a fine view of Cork Harbour and its islands, with the open sea beyond.

Prison Visit
Cork City Gaol and Radio Museum (Sunday's Well Road; tel: 021-430 5022; www.corkcitygaol. com; daily Mar–Oct 9.30am–5pm, Nov–Feb 10am–4pm; charge) occupies an imposing castle-like building high above the city on the northwestern side. The austere Victorian gaol is inhabited by life-size characters, each with a sad story to tell. The quaint Radio Museum in the Governor's House displays genuine artefacts that illustrate the history of the early days of Irish and international radio communication.

Food & Drink

③ **JACOB'S LADDER**
Water's Edge Hotel, Cobh; tel: 021-481 5566; www.watersedgehotel.ie; daily B, L and D; €–€€
Jacob's Ladder is a clean-lined, contemporary bar-restaurant featuring a mesmerising panoramic harbour view. This is complemented by a varied and imaginative menu with an Irish accent: baked ham with parsley sauce, for example. It's also a great place to come for a coffee or a cocktail.

7

WEST CORK COAST

Spend a day exploring the rural coastline of west County Cork, starting in Kinsale, a historic port turned fashionable resort, then meandering along coastal roads and through quiet countryside to the sheltered waters and lush vegetation of Bantry Bay and Glengarriff.

DISTANCE 136km (85 miles)
TIME A full day
START Charles Fort, Kinsale
END Glengarriff
POINTS TO NOTE

A car is essential for this tour. At the end, either return to Kinsale on the R586 from Bantry (88km/54 miles) or push on 27km (17 miles) to Kenmare, or 80km (50 miles) to Killorglin, on the Ring of Kerry (tour 8).

Below: Charles Fort.

Once a run-down rural backwater, west Cork coast's proximity to Cork Airport, its friendly people and its unspoilt environment have led many to buy holiday homes in the area, while others have relocated permanently, bringing prosperity to the region. This drive heads west, skirting rocky headlands.

KINSALE

Charles Fort
Approaching Kinsale from Cork, look out for a signpost to **Charles Fort** ❶ (tel: 021-477 2263; www.heritage ireland.ie; daily mid-Mar–Oct 10am–6pm, Nov–mid-Mar until 5pm; charge), 2km (1 mile) outside town on the outer harbour. This massive star-shaped fort encloses 3 ha (8 acres) of land and was built in 1680. In clear weather you can see the **Old Head of Kinsale**, the western extremity of the beautiful fjord-like harbour. Drive north along the coast road into town.

Kinsale Town
Kinsale ❷, 29km (18 miles) south of Cork city, overlooks the estuary of the Bandon River. Its narrow streets and tall

Georgian houses are clustered around the sides of a conical hill. Before becoming a fashionable resort famous for its restaurants, Kinsale was best known for the Battle of Kinsale (1601), in which the combined forces of the (Catholic) Irish and Spanish armies were defeated by the (Protestant) English. After this rout the Irish clan chiefs left for Europe and never returned.

Park on the quay, walk up Pearse Street and then turn left then right for **Desmond Castle**, a 15th-century tower house, containing the **International Museum of Wine** (Cork Street, tel: 021-477 4855; www.heritageireland.ie; mid-Apr–mid-Sept daily 10am–6pm; charge). The museum celebrates the Irish families who took up winemaking after leaving for France in the 17th century; their names may be familiar: Hennessy, Barton, Lynch, Dillon...

Check out Kinsale's reputation for high-quality food by having breakfast or lunch at **Cucina**, see ⑪①.

THE ROAD TO SKIBBEREEN

The R600 crosses the River Bandon heading west to quieter country where a slow pace of life prevails. The road follows a wide sea inlet to **Timoleague** ❸, a sleepy village where the ruins of a 14th-century **Franciscan friary** overlook the estuary.

Drombeg Stone Circle
You will only glimpse **Clonakilty** ❹, a pretty market town with traditional wooden shop fronts and carefully tended floral displays, as you bypass it

Above from far left: Kinsale; brightly painted house; lighthouse at the Old Head of Kinsale; shop fronts in Kinsale.

Food and Drink

① CUCINA
9 Market Street, Kinsale, tel: 021-470 0707; www.cucina.ie; B, L and AT; D Thur–Sat; €
The best cappuccino in town is served in a smartly designed contemporary café. Daily specials – paninis, pastas and salads – are light and imaginative, using, for example, goat's cheese, rocket and local charcuterie.

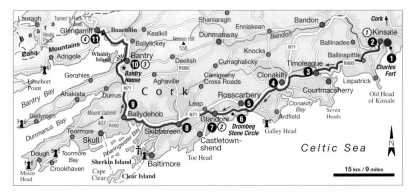

Celtic Sea

15 km / 9 miles

Lighthouse Visit

If you like lighthouses, detour 22.5km (14 miles) southwest from Ballydehob on the R592 to the Mizen Head Visitor Centre (tel: 028-35115; www.mizenhead.net; mid-Mar–Oct daily 10.30am–5pm, winter Sat–Sun 11am–4pm only; charge). The centre is in the lighthousekeeper's house on an island at the tip of the rocky peninsula, accessed by a suspension bridge.

Below: lobster nets.

on the N71. On the inlet at **Rosscarbery ⑤**, flocks of swans glide by. About 200m/yds further on, take the R597 west (left) for Glandore. After about 5km (3 miles) a sign leads to **Drombeg Stone Circle ⑥**, sited on a plateau facing the distant sea. This is one of the most complete of the region's mysterious early Bronze Age remains. A burial, carbon-dated to 1124–794BC, was excavated at the centre of the ring of 14 stones, but nobody knows who built the circle or what it signified to them. Locally, it is believed to be in alignment with the setting sun at the winter solstice. Beside it is a Bronze Age cooking pit, with full instructions.

Millionaire's Row

Continue west to **Glandore ⑦**, a line of south-facing houses perched on top of a cliff, nicknamed 'Millionaire's Row'. There is a magical view over a pair of islands to the open sea beyond. In sunny weather it is hard to resist an outdoor drink; try **Hayes' Bar**, see ⑪②.

Skibbereen

Follow the narrow road through Glandore along the wooded estuary, rejoining the N71 at **Leap**. Continue west to **Skibbereen ⑧**, a small market town, once a major junction on the West Cork Railway. The tiny **Skibbereen Heritage Centre** (Upper Bridge Street; tel: 028-40900; www. skibbheritage.com; mid-May–mid-Sept daily 10am–6pm, mid-Sept–mid-May Tue–Sat; charge) explains the Great Famine of 1845–9, which took the lives of over 100,000 people locally.

As it approaches **Ballydehob ⑨**, a brightly painted hill village, the N71 turns inland and climbs across remote, sparsely inhabited hills, some planted with Sitka spruce, before winding down to gentler climes.

BANTRY BAY

Bantry ⑩, a quiet seaport and market town, is at the southeastern corner of the bay of the same name. The rafts that you see on the bay are evidence of the biggest local industry: mussel farming. You can sample the product

in town at **O'Connor's Seafood Restaurant**, see ③.

Bantry House and Garden (tel: 027-50047; www.bantryhouse.ie; mid-Mar–Oct daily 10am–6pm; charge) is set on a height overlooking the 6.5km (4 mile) wide bay and the serried ranks of surrounding mountains. The large mid-18th-century mansion is well worth a visit. Its interior contains a fine selection of treasures brought back by the first Earl of Bantry from his Grand Tour of Europe in the early 19th century, while the extensive garden has steep stone terraces, formal parterres, venerable wisteria and a walled garden.

Glengarriff & Garinish Island
Beyond Bantry, the N71 runs along the water's edge through wooded **Ballylickey**, rising to a height above Bantry Bay, where there are several viewing points. Then it's downhill again to **Glengarriff** ⓫, a sheltered inlet at the top of the bay with a sub-tropical climate. The harbour here is presided over by the **Glengarriff Eccles Hotel**, see 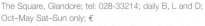④.

Continue into the village and park near Quills Woollen Mills. Beside the public toilets is a kiosk selling tickets for **boat trips** from the Blue Pool ferry point. Choose between an hour-long **harbour trip**, with close-up views of basking seals, or a visit to **Garinish Island** (also known as Illnacullin; tel: 027-63040; www.heritageireland.ie; Apr–Sept Mon–Sat 10am–6.30pm,

Sun 1–6.30pm, June–Aug Sun from 11am, Oct Sun 1–5pm; entry charge in addition to ferry; café), 10 minutes offshore. In the early 20th century the 15ha (37 acres) of land on the island were transformed into a series of formal and informal gardens, using unusual shrubs and rare subtropical flowers, the whole framed by the rocky peaks of the surrounding hills.

For a scenic walk, drive through the busy village to **Glengarriff Woods Nature Reserve** (www.npws.ie), where there are a number of way-marked trails.

Food & Drink

② HAYES' BAR

The Square, Glandore; tel: 028-33214; daily B, L and D; Oct–May Sat–Sun only; €
This simple local has a superb bay view and offers a surprising range of wines by the glass. Local prawns, crab and salmon are served in open sandwiches and West Cork farmhouse cheese features in the *croque monsieur*. Tapas are served until 9pm.

③ O'CONNOR'S SEAFOOD RESTAURANT

The Square, Bantry; tel: 027-55664; www.oconnorseafood. com; Mon–Wed and Sat D, Thur–Fri L and D; €€–€€€
This superb town centre restaurant offers up a shoal of seafood delights, including chowder, oysters, calamari, fresh lobster by the pound and mussels prepared in three different ways. Meat eaters and vegetarians are also catered for.

④ GLENGARRIFF ECCLES HOTEL

Glengarriff Harbour; tel: 027-63003; www.eccleshotel.com; B, L and D; €–€€
All kinds of notable writers have stayed here, from William Thackeray to W.B. Yeats to Virginia Woolf. The food is standard hotel/bar fare, but you should visit this large 250-year-old hotel for its splendid location overlooking Glengarriff Harbour and the atmosphere of Victorian grandeur that persists.

THE RING OF KERRY

The Ring of Kerry is one of Europe's great scenic drives, a circular route around the rim of the Iveragh Peninsula, through rugged sandstone hills and lush sub-tropical vegetation, with myriad mountain and coastal views.

DISTANCE 140km (87 miles)
TIME 1 or 2 days
START Killorglin
END Kenmare
POINTS TO NOTE

A car is essential to tour the Ring independently. Tour bus traffic leaves Killarney 16km (10 miles) east of Killorglin between 9am and 10am travelling anti-clockwise, so leave earlier or later. Showery weather can add dramatic light effects, but if the forecast is for heavy rain, make other plans. Allow two days if you intend to visit the Skellig Rocks, a 3–4 hour boat trip; book ahead and bear in mind the ferry leaves Portmagee at 10.30am.

The Ring of Kerry follows the coast of the Iveragh Peninsula in the extreme southwest. The route overlooks Dingle Bay to the north, the open Atlantic to the west and the sheltered waters of Kenmare Bay to the south. Inland, to the east, are the purple hills known as Macgillycuddy's Reeks and the Lakes of Killarney *(see p.63)*. The Gulf Stream ensures a mild, frost-free climate.

DINGLE BAY

At **Killorglin ❶** on the River Laune join the Ring of Kerry (N70) by driving west across the river and up the steep main street. This market town is known for its annual Puck Fair, a street festival held in August (see www.puckfair.ie).

Kerry Bog Village Museum

The scenery begins about 8km (5 miles) beyond Killorglin amid wild, sparsely inhabited hills. Stop at the **Red Fox Inn** for the **Kerry Bog Village Museum ❷** (tel: 066-976 9184; www.kerrybogvillage.ie; daily 9am–6pm; charge), three reconstructed cottages with turf fires, ponies and dogs. It commemorates a simple rural lifestyle which persisted until the mid-20th century.

Rossbeigh

Just beyond tiny **Glenbeigh**, detour 2km (1¼ miles) on the R564 to **Rossbeigh ❸**, a 6.5km (4 mile) sandy beach facing north across Dingle Bay. Take a few minutes to get your bearings and enjoy the sea air. After Glenbeigh the road curves dramatically towards the coast, following a cliff top between the mountains and the pounding Atlantic.

Cahirciveen

Cahirciveen ❹ is the chief market town of south Kerry, but usually has a deserted air, even over 150 years after being devastated by the Famine. Park near the **Tourist Information Office** (Church Street; tel: 066-947 1300) and walk down the side road to the **Old Barracks** (tel: 066-947 2777; Mon–Fri 10am–4.30pm, Sat 11.30am–4.30pm, Sun 1–5pm; charge), an exotic white turreted building that once housed the local constabulary. Restored as a Heritage Centre, it has informative displays on local history, including the Famine. From here, you can see the estuary of the Carhen River, the more attractive side of town. Back at the main road turn west to the **O'Connell Memorial Church**, a huge Gothic-style edifice with a black limestone facade, built in 1888. Across the road is **Gallery One**, showcasing the work of the local craft co-op. Further down is **QC's**, see ⑪① *(p.62)*, a good spot for a break.

Above: coastal view on the Ring of Kerry.

The Liberator

Daniel O'Connell (1775–1847), 'the Liberator', was born in Cahirciveen and adopted by an uncle from whom he inherited an estate at Derrynane. Landowner, lawyer and orator, he dominated Irish politics in the early 19th century. Educated in France (as were many wealthy Catholics), he introduced democracy to Ireland and was responsible for the Catholic Emancipation Act of 1829, allowing Catholics and Dissenters to vote, enter the professions and own land. Tall, burly and inexhaustible, O'Connell's immense appetite and physical stamina were legendary. He was no saint; he fought a fatal duel in his youth and had a reputation as a womaniser (all of which endeared him to the people). Most Irish towns and villages have an O'Connell Street, including Dublin *(see p.35).*

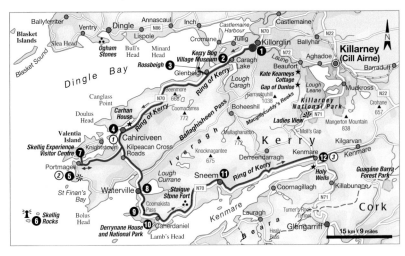

Valentia Island
Between April and September turn right at Reenard Cross for the Valentia Island Ferry (tel: 066-947 6141; daily 8.30am–10.30pm; charge) to Knightstown, an attractive 18th-century village. Valentia (pop. 700) is a peaceful place, good for walks.

ATLANTIC COAST

As you leave Cahirciveen, the **Valentia Observatory**, now part of the Irish meteorological service, is on the right. It was originally sited on Valentia Island *(see margin)* in 1868, because the island had a telegraphic link to London and was in the path of most weather systems coming in from the Atlantic.

Portmagee & Skellig Rocks

Shortly beyond the observatory, head west for 12km (7½ miles) to **Portmagee ❺**, a tiny fishing village and the departure point for the boat trip to Skellig Rocks. **The Bridge Bar** here is perfect for a bowl of seafood chowder, see ⑪②.

Weather permitting, small open boats make the 13km (8 mile) crossing from Portmagee to **Skellig Rocks ❻** (leaves 10.30am; tel: 066-947 6142; www.skel ligexperience.com/boats) in about an hour. **Little Skellig** is home to over 27,000 gannets, while **Skellig Michael** (where landing is permitted) rises to a double peak 217m (712ft) high. Over 500 stone steps lead to a simple monastery, its dry-stone buildings clinging to the cliff-edge, as they have done since the 7th century.

If you are unable to take the boat trip, drive across the causeway to **Valentia Island** to visit the **Skellig Experience Visitor Centre ❼** (tel: 066-947 6306; www.skelligexperience.com; Apr–Nov daily 10am–6pm; charge), which introduces the Unesco-listed Skellig Michael and the other rocks.

Waterville

Return to the main Ring road and drive south 11km (7 miles) to **Waterville ❽**, a small resort famous for its golf course and the game angling on Lough Currane. Park in the centre near the Butler Arms and statue of Charlie Chaplin, who used to holiday here, and take a walk on the windswept sandy beach.

Derrynane House

Stop at the parking area on the **Coomakista Pass ❾** to enjoy views of the

Food & Drink

① QC'S
Church Street, Cahirciveen; tel: 066-947 2244; www.qcbar.com; daily, L and D, Easter–mid-Oct; €€–€€€
A culinary highlight of Kerry, this award-winning seafood restaurant serves fish from its own fleet of trawlers, and local game in season. At the western end of town on the main (N70) road.

② THE BRIDGE BAR
Portmagee; tel: 066-947 7108; www.moorings.ie; daily L and D, Oct–Apr no food served on Mon; €
Located right on the seafront, with a rustic pine interior warmed by an open fire. The simply prepared fish is leaping fresh; alternatively, opt for the roast of the day.

③ THE PARK HOTEL
Kenmare; tel: 064-664 1200; www.parkkenmare.com; daily lounge noon–6pm, dining room D; €€–€€€€
Kenmare is the foodie capital of southwest Ireland and the Park is the jewel in its crown. The elegant dining room, built in 1897 by the Great Southern Railway, is imposing but friendly. Food is light but flavoursome, featuring seafood and local specialities, such as Kerry lamb and Skeghanore duck. The bar and lounge serve a lighter menu during the day.

Above from far left:
three aspects of
Killarney: Ladies'
View, farmhouse
crockery at Muckross
Traditional Farms,
Lough Leane.

Skelligs to the west and the mountains of the Beara Peninsula to the south.

In **Caherdaniel** drive downhill to **Derrynane House and National Park** ❿ (tel: 066-947 5113; www.heritage ireland.ie; Apr and Oct–late Nov Wed–Sun 10.30am–5pm, May–Sept daily 10.30am–6pm; charge), family home of Daniel O'Connell *(see feature, p.61)*. The modest 1702 manor house is furnished with heirlooms. Walk along the sheltered beach and explore the rock pools.

KENMARE RIVER

The Kenmare River is a sea inlet that divides the Iveragh Peninsula from the Beara Peninsula in the south.

Sneem

Brightly painted **Sneem** ⓫ has two village greens; park by the second. Walk down the road beyond the Blue Bull (signposted 'Pier') for about 300m/yds past an attractive garden. Looking back through the reeds you can appreciate Sneem's sheltered location between the sea and the hills. Note the difference in vegetation on this side of the Ring; in the place of bare windswept rocks is a lush growth of trees and shrubs.

Kenmare

Follow the N70 east for 27km (17 miles) to **Kenmare** ⓬. Laid out in 1755 in a triangle, the compact village is packed with restaurants, boutiques and crafts shops. Park in its centre beside the green and the **Kenmare Heritage Centre** (tel: 064-664 1223), which introduces the town's history. There is a lively restaurant scene in Kenmare's centre, but for somewhere really memorable try **The Park Hotel**, see ⓣ③, just outside of town, a left turn off the N71 towards Bantry.

Killarney

Killarney was a magnet for tourists even before Queen Victoria's 1861 visit. Avoid today's tour-bus trade by spending as much time as possible exploring the heather-clad mountains and as little as possible in the town centre. For the full impact of the glacially formed chain of sparkling blue lakes, arrive on the N71 and stop at Ladies' View.

Killarney National Park is a car-free zone and Muckross Park is at its core. Travel in traditional style by hiring a jaunting car (open horse-drawn carriage) at the park gates: the 'jarveys' (drivers) are famous for their talk, although nowadays you will also hear their mobile phone ringing. The park has wild deer, walking trails, a lakeside manor and Muckross Traditional Farms (www.muckross-house.ie; Apr–Oct, check website for times; charge), a beguiling outdoor museum of rural life.

For a quintessential Killarney experience, take a half-day Gap of Dunloe tour (O'Connor Autotours, Ross Road, Killarney; tel: 064-663 1052; May–Oct), which starts 19km (12 miles) to the west at Kate Kearney's Cottage and proceeds on a pony and trap or on foot through 6.5km (4 miles) of narrow, unpaved mountain passes past huge glacial boulders, returning to town by boat. End the day by watching the sun set over the lakes from the 7th-century monastic ruins at Aghadoe. For more details of all things Killarney, contact the Tourist Information Office (Beech Road, Killarney; tel: 064-663 1633; www.corkkerry.ie).

THE DINGLE PENINSULA

Jutting out into the Atlantic, the Dingle Peninsula is Europe's most westerly point. The Irish-speaking area at its tip is rich in prehistoric and early Christian remains, and has rugged cliffs and sandy beaches. Finish by crossing the sensational Conor Pass to Tralee, capital of County Kerry.

Dingle Way
The Dingle Way (Slí Chorca Dhuibhne; www.dingleway.net), a way-marked walking route, starts and ends in Tralee, taking about eight days to complete the 179km (111 miles). It crosses the peninsula from Camp to Annascaul, passing through Dingle Town, then the cliff scenery of the Slea Head area to the slopes of Mount Brandon.

DISTANCE 125km (77½ miles)
TIME A full day
START Castlemaine
END Tralee
POINTS TO NOTE

There is a daily bus service from Tralee to Dingle town, but really a car is essential for this tour. Avoid the Conor Pass in misty weather; take the N86 from Dingle all the way to Tralee. Note, there isn't a petrol station or ATM west of Dingle town.

Adare (tour 10) is situated 84km (52 miles) northeast of Tralee on the N21 Limerick road.

Begin at Castlemaine, the southern gateway to the Dingle Peninsula (Corca Dhuibhne), which stretches for some 48km (30 miles) from Tralee in the east to Slea Head in the west.

CASTLEMAINE TO DINGLE

Some 10km (6 miles) beyond **Castlemaine ❶**, the sea comes into view as the road skirts Castlemaine Harbour. The first hint of the scenery to come is at **Inch ❷**, where a 6.5km (4 mile) long sand spit backed by dunes stretches out into Dingle Bay. Stop for a bracing walk along the unusual west-facing beach and refuel at **Sammy's**, see ⑪①.

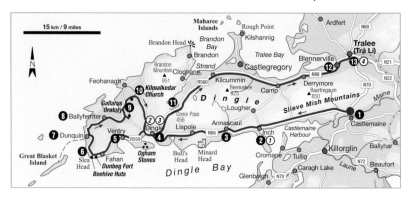

Annascaul

The wide road at **Annascaul ❸**, where the Castlemaine and Tralee roads meet, was once the location of a major cattle fair, which is also why this tiny village has so many pubs. One such pub, the **South Pole Inn** (tel: 066-915 2626), was built by Tom Crean (1877–1938), a local man of legendary strength who enlisted in the Royal Navy and served on three Antarctic expeditions, with both Scott and Shackleton. The pub is crammed with fascinating memorabilia, and you can enjoy a view of green hills and grazing sheep from its front door.

Dingle Town & Harbour

From Annascaul, it's 17km (10½ miles) west to **Dingle ❹** (An Daingean). Turn left at the entrance and park on the pier. Dingle has a population of about 1,500, which can treble in summer. Its fame was spread by the filming of *Ryan's Daughter* in 1969, and again in 1983 by the arrival of a dolphin, Fungie, who still plays in the harbour mouth. A bronze statue on the pier pays homage to the wild visitor. Opposite, in a humble tin shed, is one of Dingle's best seafood restaurants, **Out of the Blue**, see ⑪②.

A triangular 10-minute walk from the pier up Green Street, down Main Street and back along the Mall will take you past most of the town's shops and restaurants. The better craft shops are at the top of Green Street. Across the road from the pier you will find **Chowder Café**, see ⑪③.

SLEA HEAD DRIVE

Head west for 6km (3¼ miles) on the R559 to **Ventry ❺** (Ceann Trá), an Irish-speaking village with a few pubs and shops. The bay here has a long sandy beach and safe swimming.

Between Ventry and Slea Head there are over 400 small conical huts of un-mortared stone known as beehive huts. While some date from the 5th–8th centuries and were used by hermit monks, many were built in the early 20th century to house farm implements; timber is so scarce here that it is cheaper to build with stone.

Above from far left:
Dingle Harbour;
pubs and restaurants
in town.

Food & Drink

① SAMMY'S STORE AND CAFÉ
Inch Beach; tel: 066-915 8118; daily Mar–Oct, weekends only Nov–Feb; B, L and D; €
Sammy's has an amazing location right on the beach, and has a child-friendly café as well as a bar. By day it serves simple but freshly prepared salads, burgers, soups and sandwiches, while at night the menu features fresh fish and steaks.

② OUT OF THE BLUE
The Pier, Dingle town; tel: 066-915 0811; Mon–Sun D, Sun L; closed Nov–Feb; €€–€€€
It's a basic tin hut beside the pier, but it serves the freshest of seafood. Lobster, John Dory, brill, black sole and even the humble mackerel are cooked to perfection. Book in advance to avoid disappointment.

③ CHOWDER CAFÉ
Strand Street, Dingle town; tel: 066-915 1061; daily L and D, L only Oct–May. €–€€
A simple 12-table café where bread, cakes and desserts are all home-made. There are also good vegetarian and gluten-free options, including locally reared steaks, slow-cooked lamb shank and excellent chips.

Above from left:
Slea Head; Ventry bay.

Ogham Stones
These are carved with letters from the early medieval Ogham alphabet in which the letters are made up of parallel lines and notches.

Below: Conor Pass.

Dunbeg Fort

About 6km (3¾ miles) further, stop at the distinctive Stone House Restaurant at **Fahan** to visit **Dunbeg Promontory Fort** (tel: 066-915 9755; www.dunbeg fort.com; Apr–Oct daily 10am–5pm; charge), a defensive promontory fort that was inhabited during about 800–1200AD. A short film introduces the compact site, which has an inner dry-stone rampart and a souterrain. It is perched right on the cliff's edge, reached by a short downhill path beside a field grazed by donkeys. About 250m/yds on, park again to visit a group of **beehive huts** above the road (charge). In fine weather you can look south across the sea to the Skellig Rocks *(see p.62)*, where hardy monks lived in similar shelters.

Slea Head

The road climbs west around Eagle Mountain to **Slea Head ❻** (Ceann Sléibhe), marked by a life-size roadside Crucifixion. **Coumenole**, the sandy beach below, will be familiar from *Ryan's Daughter (see also p.65)*. It looks tempting, but swimming here is dangerous.

Dunquin & the Blasket Islands

Nearby **Dunquin ❼** (Dún Chaoin) is a scattered settlement, as was the tradition in old Gaelic Ireland. The **Great Blasket** (An Blascaod Mór) is the largest of seven islands visible offshore. It was inhabited until 1953 by a tough, self-sufficient community of farmers and fishermen. The **Great Blasket Centre** (tel: 077-915 6444; www.heri tageireland.ie; daily 10am–6pm, July–Aug until 7pm; charge) at Dunquin explains the islanders' heritage. From **Dunquin Pier** you can catch a ferry to the island *(see margin, right)*.

Gallarus Oratory

Continue on the R559 for 7km (4⅓ miles) to Irish-speaking **Ballyferriter ❽** (Baile an Fheirtéaraigh), the largest village (two shops and four pubs that serve simple food) on this side of the peninsula, founded by the Norman Ferriter family in the 12th century and popular today with holidaymakers and Irish-language enthusiasts.

Some 8km (5 miles) further on is the **Gallarus Oratory ❾** (visitor centre: tel: 066-915 5333, charge; oratory: free)

This extraordinary 8th-century building of unmortared stone is shaped like an inverted boat, and remains as dry and solid as the day it was built.

At the crossroads north of Gallarus, turn right (east) for the ruined **Kilmalkedar Church** ⓾. It was built around 1150, although the settlement dates from the 7th century. The superbly carved Romanesque features have hardly weathered over the years. There are a number of interesting standing stones nearby, including a sundial stone and several Ogham stones *(see left)*.

CONOR PASS TO TRALEE

Return to Dingle on the R559 (8km/5 miles). If the weather is fine, drive to Tralee via the **Conor Pass** ⓫ (48km/30 miles), a rocky mountain road that crosses the peninsula from south to north. It rises steeply to 456m (1,496ft) above sea level, and parts are so narrow that you must negotiate right of way with oncoming traffic. It is not for the faint-hearted, but it does offer spectacular vistas of Brandon Bay and the wide Atlantic ocean in the north; stop in a lay-by to enjoy the view. The road then corkscrews down to the bay, past a dazzling waterfall and boulder-strewn hillsides studded with glittering lakes.

Blennerville

There are glimpses of the sea as you drive along the R560 and join the N86 at **Camp**. **Blennerville** ⓬ is a mainly Georgian village perched between Tralee Bay and the old ship canal. It still has a large working windmill, best viewed from a distance.

Tralee

County town of Kerry, **Tralee** ⓭ (Trá Lí) has a population of 35,000, many of whom are students. Park in the centre near the town park beside **Ashe Memorial Hall**, an imposing neoclassical building, housing the **Tourist Information Office** (tel: 066-712 1288). The front entrance leads to the **Kerry County Museum** (tel: 066-712 7777; www.kerrycountymuseum.ie; June–Aug daily 9.30am–5.30pm, Sept–May Tue–Sat only; charge), with a lively display of Kerry's history from ancient times. Denny Street leads from the museum to the centre and contains the best of Tralee's Georgian architecture, mostly now lawyers' offices. A pedestrian alley on the left of Denny Street leads to Tralee's pedestrian piazza, which usually has a few market stalls trading. If you are in need of refreshment, try **The Grand Hotel**, see ⓸④, back on Denny Street.

Blasket Trips

Dunquin Pier is a steep concrete footpath that spirals down to the sea, where *curraghs* (canoes covered in tarred canvas) are stored upside-down. A modern ferry (tel: 066-915 6422; www.blasketisland.com) makes the 20-minute crossing to Great Blasket Island, weather-permitting, a number of times a day between Easter and October. Walk through the island's deserted village and along narrow cliff paths rich in wildlife, and watch the seals on White Strand.

Food & Drink

④ THE GRAND HOTEL

Denny Street, Tralee; tel: 066-712 1499; www.grandhotel tralee.com; B, L and D; €–€€

At the centre of Tralee, this fine old institution, with its imposing Victorian facade, is a popular spot all day long. In the Pikeman's Bar there are good-value specials at the self-service lunch like roast leg of lamb or sea trout fillet. More formal food is served in the evening in Samuel's Restaurant.

LIMERICK & SHANNON

On this drive, explore the charming village of Adare, wander the medieval streets of Limerick and then head into the castle country around the Shannon estuary to discover more of Ireland's past at Bunratty Castle and Folk Park.

DISTANCE 71km (44 miles)
TIME A full day
START Adare
END Quin
POINTS TO NOTE

Adare is on the N21, 7km (4 miles) west of the N20 Cork–Limerick road and 17km (10 miles) southwest of Limerick city. From Quin, return to the N18, where you can head south for Limerick (34km/21 miles) or north for Lahinch (38km/23 miles), the starting point of tour 11.

Limerick History
Founded by the Vikings in 812, Limerick takes its name from the Norse word, *laemrich*, 'rich land'. Following the death of the King of Munster, the Normans captured Limerick in 1194, building extensive city walls; shortly after, King John ordered an imposing fortification to be built on King's Island, now the historic centre. In the 18th century Limerick extended further south with the construction of Newtown Pery, its Georgian quarter. The city went into decline after the founding of the Irish Free State in 1922, and suffered heavy emigration and much urban poverty; a phase evoked in Frank McCourt's memoir, *Angela's Ashes*. The city's recovery began with the opening of Shannon Airport in 1945.

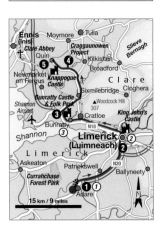

The Limerick region and the Shannon estuary have been of great strategic importance ever since the Vikings established a sheltered seaport on an island at the head of the Shannon estuary in the 9th century, which grew into the city of Limerick. During the 12th–15th centuries several monastic orders settled in the area, while Irish clan chieftains built fortified homes among the low hills and lakes to the northwest of Limerick. This castle country is dotted with the ruins of tower houses, some of which have been restored, such as Craggaunowen and magnificent Bunratty Castle.

ADARE

Begin the day to the southwest of Limerick city at **Adare ❶**, which boasts of being 'Ireland's prettiest village'. It's a tiny place and you cannot miss the **Adare Heritage Centre** (Main Street; tel: 061-396666; www.adareheritagecentre.ie; daily 9am–6pm; charge) at its heart. There is a large car park behind the centre, plus several crafts shops and a restaurant within. You can pick up a map of the village here.

Main Street

Turn left out of the Heritage Centre to the former **Trinitarian priory**, founded in 1230; it was converted into a Catholic parish church in 1811. The opposite side of the wide main street is lined by thatched cottages with flower-filled front gardens. They were built in 1830 by the local landlord, the Earl of Dunraven, for his workers. Today, most of them are either restaurants or craft shops. **Lucy Erridge's** (tel: 061-396898) is the most interesting of the latter, while the **Dunraven Arms**, see ①①, a traditional coaching inn-turned luxury hotel, is a good spot for breakfast or lunch.

Augustinian Friary

Turn left out of the Dunraven Arms, which marks the end of the village, and continue about 50m/yds to the former **Augustinian friary**, now Adare's Anglican church. To the north of the church are the well-preserved cloisters of the 1315 monastery. The church's nave and choir are also 14th-century.

The main gates of **Adare Manor** (www.adaremanor.com) are across the road from the church. The manor, which was enlarged in the Tudor Revival style in the mid-19th century, is now a luxury hotel and golf resort.

River Walk

At this point you could go through the metal stile beside the Anglican church for a lovely rural riverside walk of about 1.5km (1 mile). The walk follows the banks of the River Maigue, rich in wildlife, to the west, before looping back to the village centre down Station Road.

LIMERICK CITY

Leaving Adare for **Limerick ❷** takes you out of a cosy time warp and into modern Ireland, with a dual carriageway (N20) approaching the Republic's third largest city. The bulk of the low-lying city lies on the eastern bank of the River Shannon, and the wide, fast-flowing river is its best asset.

Follow signs for the centre and Arthur's Quay car park; behind is the **Tourist Information Centre** (tel: 061-317522; www.limerick.ie; Mon–Sat 9am–6pm, July–Aug daily). Both the Shannon and, to the east, King John's Castle can be seen from here.

Hunt Museum

Turn right up Francis Street and left into Rutland Street for the **Hunt Museum Ⓐ** (tel: 061-312833; www.hunt museum.com; Mon–Sat 10am–5pm, Sun 2–5pm; charge). Once the city's

Above from far left: Adare's former Augustinian friary; thatched cottage in 'Ireland's prettiest village'; King John Castle in Limerick.

Below: idyllic Adare.

Food & Drink

① DUNRAVEN ARMS

Main Street, Adare; tel: 061-605900; www.dunraven-hotel.com; daily; B, L and D; €–€€

Now one of Ireland's leading hotels, the Dunraven Arms has not forgotten its origins as a village inn. Sample a coffee and scone or a light lunch in its traditional bar or bright, modern conservatory with a garden view.

Custom House, the compact Georgian building has the finest collection of Celtic and medieval treasures outside Dublin's National Museum, plus a small selection of Irish and European paintings, including works by Renoir and Picasso. Once a private collection, it was donated to the nation in 1976 by the Hunt family. There's also a shop and an excellent café overlooking the river.

St Mary's Cathedral

Turn left upon leaving the Hunt Museum and cross a bridge over a tributary of the Shannon to **King's Island**, site of the city's original settlement. On the left is **St Mary's Cathedral ❸**

(tel: 061-310293; www.cathedral.lim erick.anglican.org; daily 9am–5pm, Nov–Feb until 1pm). The rounded Romanesque entrance door is a remnant of its origins as a 12th-century palace belonging to Donal Mór O'Brien, King of Munster. Much of the compact cruciform building dates from the 15th-century, such as the black-oak misericords with carved animal features in the choir stalls.

King John's Castle

From the cathedral turn onto Nicholas Street and walk north for **King John's Castle ❻** (tel: 061-411201, www.shan nonheritage.com; daily 10am–5pm last admission 4pm; charge), a massive fortification with curtain walls and two drum towers, built by the Normans in the 1200s and rebuilt and extended many times over the years. The outdoor courtyard gives access to the massive bastions and views of the river and city.

Riverside Footpath

Turn right out of the castle, and right again down a pedestrian alley beside the castle walls, past the **Jim Kemmy Municipal Museum** (tel: 061-417826; summer Mon–Sat 10am–5pm, Sun 2–5pm, winter Tue–Sat only; free), to return to the car park along a riverside footpath. At Merchant's Quay look for the modern white footbridge across the river; alternatively, walk up to the road bridge for refreshments at **The Locke Bar and Bistro**, see ⑪②.

City of Youth

One reason why there are so many young people in Limerick is due to its university (www.ul.ie), a thriving institution founded in 1972, which currently has 11,000 students and 1,300 staff. Its campus at Plassey, 3km/1¾ miles from city centre off the N24 (Waterford road), is a showcase for contemporary architecture and design.

Cross the River Shannon in County Clare via the N18, the road to Shannon Airport and the west of Ireland.

Bunratty Castle & Folk Park

Impressively big, **Bunratty Castle ❸** (tel: 061-360788; www.shannonheritage.com; daily 9am–4pm; charge) has a square tower at each corner and a drawbridge. Dating largely from the 16th-century, it contains furniture and tapestries from the 14th–17th centuries. In the evening Bunratty hosts 'medieval banquets' – a meal with Irish cabaret and plenty of 'Blarney'.

The extensive **Folk Park** (as above with last entry 4.15pm, June–Aug Sat–Sun until 6pm, last entry 5.15pm) consists of 10ha (25 acres) of re-constructed traditional dwellings, including a typical village street *c.*1880, complete with pecking hens. The original of many an 'Irish pub', **Durty Nelly's** (tel: 061-364861) squats on the riverbank beside the castle. It does not serve food in the daytime, so turn right out of Bunratty Castle and after a short way you will see **J.P. Clarke's Country Pub**, see ⓘ③.

Craggaunowen Project

Take the narrow country lane behind J.P. Clarke's to the T-junction with the R471 and turn right for **Sixmilebridge.** Drive through the village and turn left

onto the R469 for Craggaunowen, well signposted about 10km (6 miles) from Bunratty. Among the attractions at the **Craggaunowen Project ❹** (tel: 061-360788; mid-Apr–mid-Oct daily 10am–4.15pm; charge) are a restored 1550 castle and a reconstructed *crannóg*, a fortified dwelling of clay and wattle built on a lake island.

Quin

Retrace your steps from Craggaunowen and turn west onto the R469 for about 4km (2½ miles) to **Quin ❺**. In the village centre are the well-preserved remains of a **Franciscan abbey**, founded in 1402, with cloisters and elaborate stone tombs. Across the stream are the ruins of a 13th-century church.

Drive across the village's bridge, and take the first left, a narrow country road which meanders for about 5km (3 miles) to an interchange with the N18.

Above from far left: choir stalls in St Mary's Cathedral; Guinness sign outside a Limerick pub; Hunt Museum; 9th-century Cashel Bell at the Hunt.

Food & Drink

② THE LOCKE BAR AND BISTRO

3 George's Quay, Limerick; tel: 061-413733; www.lockebar.com; daily L and D; €

A traditional riverside pub with tables outside on the tree-lined quay, the Locke is a popular place for hearty pub grub and freshly made sandwiches. There's a quieter bar upstairs with table service.

③ J.P. CLARKE'S COUNTRY PUB

Bunratty; tel: 061-363363; daily L and D; €

Escape the tour-bus trade at this stylish, modern pub close to the castle. The attractive high-ceilinged bar has an open fire and restaurant-style tables. The contemporary menu is strong on seafood; or try the beefburger with roast-pepper relish.

THE CLIFFS OF MOHER & THE BURREN

Drive along County Clare's attractive coast to the dramatic Cliffs of Moher, which rise vertically from the Atlantic, and the eerie Burren, a treeless limestone plateau that fascinates botanists, geologists and archaeologists.

DISTANCE 78km (48½ miles)

TIME A full day

START Lahinch

END Kinvara

POINTS TO NOTE

Lahinch is also spelt Lehinch. It is 30km (18½ miles) west of Ennis on the N85. Kinvara is 10km (6 miles) west of the N18 Galway–Limerick road and 30km (19 miles) south of Galway city (tour 12).

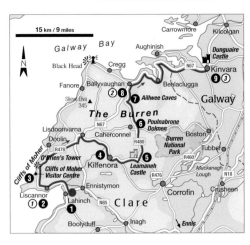

Lahinch, on the west coast of County Clare, has long been famous for its golf links and is now also one of Ireland's most popular surfing destinations. The huge bulk of the Cliffs of Moher rise 200m (650ft) straight out of the sea on this coast and stretch for some 7km (4 miles), offering distant views of the Aran Islands *(see p.78)* and close-up ones of nesting seabirds. To the north the Burren is a National Park covering 500 sq km (200 sq miles) of lunar-like limestone pavement, with unique flora and fauna and numerous megalithic remains, dating from the Stone Age and the Bronze Age, long before the arrival of the Celts.

LAHINCH TO LISCANNOR

The driving tour begins with a right turn just before **Lahinch ❶** (approaching from Ennis), but first carry straight on, turning right off the main road at the top of the village to park above the long sandy beach, where you can take a walk along its promenade. These days surfers may even outnumber golfers, and the village has a lively nightlife.

Return to the R478. The road curves north to west through the golf links and a series of sand dunes, with intermittent sea views.

Liscannor

The tiny village of **Liscannor** ❷ nearby is somewhat overwhelmed by newly built holiday homes, but still has an excellent pub at its centre, **Vaughan's Anchor Inn**, see ⑪①. The village has given its name to a black stone, Liscannor slate, usually used as flagstones, which bear the fossil remains of marine animals that lived up to 300 million years ago. In the early 20th century, over 500 men were employed in local quarries.

As you head to the Cliffs of Moher, look out for **The Rock Shop** (tel: 065-708 1930; www.therockshop.ie; daily 10am–dusk), which has interesting audio-visual displays about quarrying and a collection of antique tools.

THE CLIFFS OF MOHER

The exhilarating **Cliffs of Moher** ❸ attract over a million visitors a year. Park (charge) at the multi-million-euro **Visitor Centre** (tel: 065-708 6141; www.cliffsofmoher.ie; daily Nov–Feb 9.15am–5pm, Mar–Apr and Oct until 6.30pm, May and Sept until 7pm, June–Aug until 9.30pm; free), which is built into the hillside and roofed with grass. It contains a shop, ATM and café, plus the **Atlantic Edge Exhibition**

(charge), the highlight of which is a virtual reality tour of the cliffs from a bird's-eye view. In good weather, harpists and other buskers entertain outside. Note the extensive use of the local Liscannor stone as paving and seating.

The Cliffs

Part of the recent investment in the Cliffs of Moher included an upgrading of over 600m/yds of pathways and viewing platforms to enable visitors to enjoy the spectacle safely and without harming the area's wildlife and ecological balance. The natural layering of the rocks creates ledges that are an ideal habitat for nesting seabirds, including fulmars, kittiwakes, razorbills and puffins. The breeding season runs from May to July. For the full windswept experience, go right up to the edge and watch the waves booming far below. In clear weather you can see the Aran Islands and the far side of Liscannor Bay.

Food & Drink

① VAUGHAN'S ANCHOR INN
Liscannor; tel: 065-708 1548; daily L, AT and D; €
A reassuring aroma of fresh seafood greets you on opening the door; this traditional family-run pub is famed for its seafood, which is landed daily at the village pier. It's a child-friendly establishment, festooned with nautical bric-a-brac, with plentiful tables outside.

Above: the Cliffs of Moher.

Doolin
On a side road 5km (3 miles) north of the Cliffs of Moher, Doolin comprises a long straggle of hotels, B&Bs, hostels and restaurants, which cater to the visitors who flock here to listen to traditional music in its three pubs. O'Brien Cruises (Doolin Pier; tel: 065-707 5555; www.obrienline.com; mid-Mar–mid-Nov) offers daily sailings to the Aran Islands, and also offers a recommended one-hour cruise under the Cliffs of Moher. Booking online in advance may be cheaper than buying a ticket on the day.

Above from left: cracked limestone of the Burren; Dunguaire Castle.

Below: Poulnabrone Dolmen; ruins of Leamaneh Castle.

THE BURREN

The road now winds through the heart of the Burren, a treeless plateau with swirling limestone terraces, huge erratic rocks deposited in the Ice Age and relics of prehistoric man, including cairns, court graves, dolmens and over 400 stone forts. The land once had a thin covering of soil, but time, weather and the farming activities of pre-historic man denuded the surface, leaving the lunar-like region seen today. Meanwhile, under the ground, acid in the rainwater has seeped through the limestone to create pools and caves. Some 125 types of plant from Alpine, Arctic and Mediter-ranean zones flourish here, often growing up through the rock; they are at their best in May.

Food & Drink 🍴

② **MONK'S BAR**
Ballyvaughan; tel: 065-707 7059; daily L and D; €
Situated on the village's pier, from the outside there is an unforgettable view across Galway Bay. Inside, an open fire warms the long, low-ceilinged room, and there's a day-long menu (until 7.45pm) of soups, sandwiches, steaks, vegetarian stir-fry dishes and seafood specials.

③ **THE PIER HEAD**
The Quay, Kinvara; tel: 091-638188; L and D daily; €€
A corner bar on The Quay, with plate-glass windows offering views of Dunguaire Castle and the evening sunset across the bay, which is hugely popular locally. Sample the excellent seafood – mussels, skate and lobster – and locally sourced steak on the short but impeccably pre-pared menu.

Kilfenora

The R478 crosses the N67 outside Lisdoonvarna and becomes the R476, continuing for 9km (5¹/₂ miles) to another tiny village, **Kilfenora ❹**. Here, **St Fachtnan's Cathedral** is an attractive little 12th-century church with some finely carved effigies and three medieval high crosses. Next door, **The Burren Centre** (tel: 065-708 8030; www.theburrencentre.ie; charge) has a short film introducing the unique landscape of the Burren.

Leamaneh Castle

Continuing east, the left turn onto the R480 has an unmissable landmark, the beautifully proportioned ruins of **Leamaneh Castle ❺**. It is not open to the public and the surrounding lands are grazed by cattle. Close up, you can see that it was built in two phases: the tower in 1480 and the manor in 1640.

Poulnabrone Dolmen

The road between here and Bally-vaughan abounds in megalithic remains. A stone-walled car park has been built to accommodate visitors at the **Poulnabrone Dolmen ❻** (free), a structure over 3m (10ft) high and the Burren's finest portal tomb, dating back to 2,500BC.

Aillwee Caves

The road then winds downhill through a series of corkscrew bends, with distant sea views, to **Aillwee Caves ❼**

(065-707 7036; www.aillweecave.ie; daily 10am–5.30pm, phone in advance in Dec; charge). Fronted by a massive shop and flanked by a separate birds of prey attraction (charge), this is one of the few Burren caves accessible to the public. The guided tour takes you for about 300m/yds through narrow passages into vast stalactitic chambers and past waterfalls.

AROUND GALWAY BAY

The road skirts the southern shore of Galway Bay, a sheltered, indented coastline, and in good weather there are views of the purple hills of Connemara *(see pp.79–82)* on the opposite shore.

Ballyvaughan

A small fishing village on the southern shore of Galway Bay with plenty of accommodation, **Ballyvaughan** ❽ is the starting point of the **Burren Way** way-marked walk *(see feature)* and a popular base for walkers and scholarly visitors to the **National Park** (www.burrennationalpark.ie) on the southeastern side of the Burren. **Monk's Bar**, see ⑪②, is a waterside bar with good food and occasional live music.

Kinvara

The road east out of Ballyvaughan skirts the shore of Galway Bay, and to the right offers stunning views of the grey, rocky heights of the Burren. **Kinvara** ❾, 20km (12 miles) east, at the top of the sheltered inlet of **Kinvara Bay**, is the kind of quiet fishing village that can steal your heart away. Turn left down the road beside the Merriman Hotel and right along its harbour to see it at its best *(see also margin, right)*. Kinvara is also known for the traditional music played here, and has an excellent waterside gastropub, **The Pier Head**, see ⑪③.

Dunguaire Castle

Magnificently sited on a rock, **Dunguaire Castle** (tel: 061-360788; www.shannonheritage.com; mid-Apr–mid-Sept daily 10am–5pm, last entry 4.30pm; charge) looks out to sea on the northern side of Kinvara Bay. Built in 1520, it has been fully restored, and hosts medieval banquets in the evening (Apr–Oct; book in advance).

Galway Hookers
Beside the stone quays of Kinvara, enthusiasts tend their Galway hookers, putting a new coat of paint and a lick of tar on these traditional wooden cargo boats. They were originally designed to carry turf from Connemara across Galway Bay for cooking and fires in winter. An annual regatta, the Cruinniú na mBad, is held for the remaining boats in late August.

The Burren Way

The Burren Way runs from Ballyvaughan to Liscannor, a distance of 45km (26½ miles). The terrain varies from rocky ground where only scrub grows to magnificent wide 'green paths', and is largely off road. Part of the route runs along the top of the Cliffs of Moher, with great views of the Aran Islands. As well as a wealth of wildflowers, you might well glimpse some of the Burren fauna, which includes wild goats, foxes, hares, rabbits, badgers, the rare pine marten *(martes martes)* and a rich diversity of butterfly species.

GALWAY

A half-day walk around the medieval centre of Galway, the main urban hub of the west of Ireland and a vibrant fast-growing city with a young population and distinctive Irish identity.

DISTANCE About 1km (½ mile)

TIME A half day

START/END Eyre Square

POINTS TO NOTE

Galway city is 27km (17 miles) southeast of Oughterard, the starting point of tour 13, on the N59.

Galway city is situated where the River Corrib flows into the Atlantic Ocean. Its commercial centre is compact, largely pedestrianised and packed with quaint shops, trendy boutiques, stylish cafés and lively pubs.

Galway escaped the attention of the Vikings, thus retaining its Irish customs until the Anglo-Norman invasion in the 13th century. The invaders built a walled town, which developed as a thriving port. They traded in wine, spices and fish, forging strong links with Spain, rather than England and Wales, due to the town's westerly location. It became known as 'the City of the Tribes', as 14 powerful Anglo-Norman merchant families controlled its wealth for many centuries. Remnants of their stone-built mansions can still be seen in the city's narrow lanes and cobbled streets.

The Claddagh Ring

Galway's fishing village (long demolished) gave its name to the traditional ring with two hands holding a heart topped with a crown. The heart stands for love, the crown for loyalty and the hands for friendship. If the heart is worn pointing in, the wearer is spoken for; if it points out, he or she is still looking. The jeweller Thomas Dillon's (1 Quay Street; tel: 091-566365; www.claddaghring.ie; free) has a small claddagh ring museum.

EYRE SQUARE TO THE RIVER CORRIB

Begin at **Eyre Square ❶**, site of the **J.F. Kennedy Park** and city's focal point. In the northern corner 14 flags, each representing one of the merchant tribes, stand alongside the **Quincentennial Fountain ❷**, erected in 1984 to mark Galway's 500th anniversary as a city. Its rust-coloured 'sails' depict those of the traditional Galway hooker *(see p.75)*. The **Tourist Information Office** (091-537700; www.discoverireland.ie) is in Forster Street off the eastern corner.

The northwestern side of Eyre Square leads into **Williamsgate Street** (look for the landmark **Brown Thomas** department store; www.brownthomas.com). This street is the spine of old Galway and changes its name four times before reaching the River Corrib.

Lynch's Castle

At the junction of William Street and Shop Street, the Allied Irish Bank occupies one of Galway's oldest buildings, **Lynch's Castle ❸**, a 15th-century fortified townhouse. Note the cheeky gargoyles, Lynch family arms and the carved stone panels on its facade.

Inside, a 1651 map shows Galway's street layout, little changed today.

Collegiate Church of St Nicholas

Continue south and follow the next fork to the right, leading to the **Collegiate Church of St Nicholas ❹**, founded in 1320 and now the Church of Ireland (Episcopalian) cathedral. There is a popular belief that Christopher Columbus prayed here in 1477 before setting off to discover America. The area around the church has a vibrant Saturday market.

A signpost will direct you to Bowling Green and the **Nora Barnacle House ❺** (tel: 091-564743; mid-May–Aug Mon–Sat 9am–5pm or by appointment; charge), family home of James Joyce's wife. This tiny museum shows how an ordinary family lived in the early 20th century.

Quay Street

Return to the central spine via Lombard Street. On the corner of Cross Street and Quay Street is **Tigh Neachtain ❻** (Noctan's; tel: 091-568820; http://tighneachtain.com), one of Galway's oldest and most traditional pubs, with a warren-like wood-clad interior. It is also the unofficial information point for the city's busy arts scene.

To the left, on High Street, look for a sign to the pretty **Old Malt Arcade** and **The Malt House** restaurant, see ⓘⓘ①. To the right, on Quay Street, traditional shops selling tweeds and Aran sweaters prosper alongside vintage and designer clothing boutiques and contemporary arts-and-crafts galleries, a scene enlivened by an international array of buskers. Most bars and restaurants here, including Galway's famous fish-and-chip shop, **McDonagh's**, see ⓘ② *(p.78)*, have outside tables.

Above from far left: Spanish Arch; Quincentennial Fountain in Eyre Square; flags representing Galway's merchant tribes; one of the city's watering holes.

Food & Drink

① THE MALT HOUSE

Old Malt Arcade, 15 High Street; tel: 091-567866; www.themalthouse.ie; daily L and D; €€–€€€

A quiet restaurant set in a charming old-world courtyard, but with cool and contemporary decor and a sophisticated menu of local seafood: how about Galway Bay oysters with bacon and cabbage, or salmon in chilli broth?

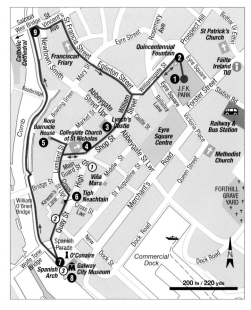

Above from left:
quayside houses in Galway; wild Connemara landscape.

Pádraic O'Conaire
A limestone statue of one of Galway's most famous literary sons was relocated from Eyre Square to the City Museum in 2006. A specialist in short stories and rural sketches, he is recognised as one of the first Modernist writers of fiction in Irish.

ALONG THE CORRIB

Quay Street reaches the Corrib at the open space of Spanish Parade. Turn left for the **Spanish Arch ❼**, named after the city's former trading partner. Beside is the new **Galway City Museum ❽** (tel: 091-532460; www.galwaycitymuseum.ie; daily 9am–5pm, Oct–May Tue–Sat only; charge), while the old stone warehouse on the water's edge houses **Ard Bia Café**, see ①③. Large flocks of swans congregate here and there are usually a few Galway hookers moored on the opposite bank.

Riverside Walk
Cross the road at Wolfe Tone Bridge and follow the footpath along this side of the river, past the William O'Brien Bridge all the way to the **Salmon Weir Bridge ❾**. From mid-April to early July, you can spot shoals of salmon lying in the water before making their way upstream to Lough Corrib to spawn. Cross the bridge to visit Galway's 20th-century **Catholic Cathedral**, before crossing back and taking the second right onto St Francis Street, which becomes Eglinton Street and leads towards Eyre Square.

Aran Islands

The Aran Islands – Inishmore (Inis Mór), Inishman (Inis Meain) and Inisheer (Inis Oirr) – are strung across the mouth of Galway Bay. They contain many archaeological remains; the biggest is Inishmore's Dun Aengus (Dún Aoinghusa), a 2,000-year-old Celtic fort perched on a 90m (300ft) sheer cliff. The islands' wildlife is unusually rich, and walkers will enjoy the Atlantic air and narrow paths that run between tiny fields. Inishmore is the most popular; go to Inishman or Inisheer for solitude. Irish is the islanders' first language, but all speak English too.

Wait until arrival to book, so you can vary your plans according to the weather. Ferries from Rossaveal take an hour and there are bus connections to Galway city. Aran Island Ferries (Tourist Information Office, Galway; tel: 091-568903; www.aranislandferries.com) has daily sailings (€25 return). Aer Arann (tel: 091-593034; www.aearannislands.ie) operates daily flights year round from Connemara Regional Airport in Inverin (€45 return). Shop around for deals including bed and breakfast; if possible, spend at least a night on an island for the full experience.

Food & Drink

② MCDONAGH'S SEAFOOD HOUSE
22 Quay Street; tel: 091-565001; www.mcdonaghs.net; restaurant Mon–Sat 5–10pm; €€
A self-service chippy (daily L and D; €) on one side and a seafood restaurant on the other, McDonagh's is a Galway institution. The chippy also offers seafood chowder and a selection of seafood salads.

③ ARD BIA CAFÉ
By Spanish Arch; tel: 091-561114; www.ardbia.com; Wed–Sun B, L, AT and D; €–€€
This compact waterside stone warehouse, with bare wooden floors and quirky art on the walls, is an atmospheric spot for a casual meal, featuring local artisan food. Pricier meals are served in the upstairs restaurant in the evening.

CONNEMARA

Drive across sparsely inhabited, lake-studded bogland, with huge skies above, mountains ahead and hospitable villages en route. Highlights include the attractive town of Clifden, Connemara National Park, the romantic 19th-century Kylemore Abbey and the deep-water fjord at Killary Harbour.

Stretching from Galway Bay in the south to Killary Harbour in the north, bordered by a rocky coastline and consisting mainly of rugged hills, wind-swept bogs and innumerable lakes, Connemara has always been an isolated place. Oscar Wilde described it as a 'savage beauty', and it remains relatively untamed. Its southern coast is home to Ireland's largest Gaeltacht (Irish-speaking area), while in north and central Connemara (covered by this tour) there are still more sheep than people; traditionally, people lived by the sea where subsistence farming could be

DISTANCE 86km (53½ miles)
TIME A full day
START Oughterard
END Leenane
POINTS TO NOTE
Oughterard is 27km (17 miles) west of Galway on the N59 Clifden road. Leenane is also on the N59, 32km (20 miles) south of Westport, the starting point of tour 14. Note that Killary Cruises offers its best rates for touring Killary Harbour if you book online.

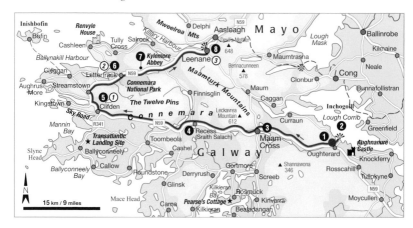

Below: a hardy Connemara pony.

augmented by fishing. The central area has largely escaped unsightly new developments, while existing attractions have been quietly enhanced.

LOUGH CORRIB

Oughterard ❶ (pronounced 'ookter-ard'), a village about 40 minutes' drive from Galway, grew up chiefly to accommodate anglers heading for Lough Corrib and consists largely of tackle shops, souvenir shops and small hotels. To orient yourself, on arriving in Oughterard turn right at the Esso petrol station for a 1km ($^1/_2$ mile) detour to the pier on **Lough Corrib** ❷. Here you can gauge the scale of the lough, which covers 17,000ha (42,000 acres) and is over 43km (26 miles) long. This is one of its widest points, at 22.5km (14 miles); Cong in County

Mayo is on the opposite shore. Today, the lough mainly attracts anglers, but in the past it was an important conduit for turf, lime, grain and seaweed to and from Galway docks.

Cruise of the Lough
Corrib Cruises (tel: 087-283 0799; www.corribcruises.com; (daily, except Tue, noon; phone in advance to confirm; charge) offers short tours of the lough from the pier as well as a day trip to **Inchagoill Island**, a romantic spot, which has interesting remains of two churches dating from the 12th and 13th centuries. The cruise continues to Cong, then direct transfers back to Oughterard.

On the western side of Oughterard is a pretty wooded stretch with a **river walk** beside the Owenriff. Enjoy the trees; they are the last you will see for many miles.

INTO CONNEMARA

About 2km (1 mile) west of Oughterard the real wilderness scenery begins: low-lying plains, scattered blue lakes and a line of distant mountains under an enormous sky usually hung with large clouds. The plains are mostly bog-land and in summer you will see heaps of hand-cut turf drying at the side of the road.

After another 14km ($8^1/_2$ miles), **Maam Cross** ❸ is more of a crossroads than a village; the junction with

the road to Leenane and the northern shores of Lough Corrib, it was an important place for trading cattle in the old days. A large agricultural fair is still held here every year in October.

Clifden

The road continues for 14km (8½ miles) to **Recess ④**, another tiny hamlet, with views in the distant north of the Twelve Bens mountain range. After another 20km (12½ miles), the road approaches **Clifden ⑤**, Connemara's main (and only) town. It is pleasantly sited, with two church spires under a wooded peak and above a sea inlet. A compact, lively place, lined with bars, cafés, bookshops and arts-and-crafts galleries, it attracts a wide range of visitors, from artists to hill climbers to Connemara pony enthusiasts. It also has a flourishing lobster fishery and a reputation for good food and comfortable lodgings. Such is its popularity that it has a one-way traffic system; go with the flow around two sides of a triangle, then park. Retrace your steps on foot to browse the shops and galleries. Look out for **Mitchell's Seafood Restaurant**, at the highest point of the triangle, see ⑪①.

Sky Road

At the western end of Market Street the road forks at the Bank of Ireland. Take the right-hand fork uphill, past the Abbeyglen Hotel, for the **Sky Road**. After about 400m/yds, look back to see Clifden, with its twin spires and the backdrop of the Twelve Bens. The road continues to rise to about 150m (500ft), with views of the beach below the town and an exhilarating panorama of the islands off Clifden Bay and the open sea beyond. People often say it feels like being on the top of the world. You can opt to drive the 11km (7 miles) circuit on narrow, twisting roads, and rejoin the N59 northwest of Clifden; this will add about half an hour to your journey.

NORTHERN CONNEMARA

Beyond Clifden, the N59 skirts for 15km (9 miles) around Connemara's western edge, and turns east for **Letterfrack ⑥**. The village has a few shops and bars, but the best place for

---

Food & Drink

① MITCHELL'S SEAFOOD RESTAURANT
Market Street, Clifden; 095-21867; Mar–Oct daily L, AT and D; €€
Stone walls, wooden floors and an open fire make an atmospheric restaurant of this former shop. Local mussels are steamed in garlic, while fresh crab is served on home-made bread. Meat eaters and vegetarians also have ample choice.

② AVOCA CRAFT SHOP
Letterfrack; tel: 095-41058; mid-Mar–early Jan daily L and AT; €
Before you even see the shop, the car park's picnic tables overlooking a sheltered sea inlet will tempt you to stop. Avoca's cafés are known for creating light, wholesome dishes, using local and artisan products. Do not miss the old-fashioned sweeties in the shop.

Above from left:
Kylemore Abbey;
wool for sale at
Leenane; Mayo
sheep; Westport
townhouses.

Coastal Garden
Drive 6km (4 miles)
west from Letterfrack
to Renvyle House (tel:
095-46100; www.ren
vyle.com; gardens:
Mar–early Jan daily
9am–5.30pm; free), a
Lutyens-style country-
house hotel at the
narrow tip of the
peninsula. It sits on
81ha (200 acres),
with the Atlantic
Ocean on either side
and a backdrop of
mountains. The
gardens have
woodland walks,
formal sections and
areas emphasising
coastal habitats.

a break is on the western approach at
the **Avoca Craft Shop**, see ①②, *(p.81)*.
Just beyond it is the **Connemara
National Park Visitor Centre** (tel:
095-41054; www.connemaranational
park.ie; mid-Mar–Oct daily 9am–
5.30pm; free). The park itself (open
year round; free) is not enclosed, but
covers some 2,000ha (4,942 acres) of
scenic wilderness. Trails have been
marked out of varying degrees of diffi-
culty. The Visitor Centre is a model of
its kind, with displays on Connemara's
history, fauna, flora and geology, a children's playground, a tea room and an
indoor picnic area.

Kylemore Abbey

Nearby, **Kylemore Abbey** ❼ (tel: 095-
41146; www.kylemoreabbey.com; car
park, exhibition rooms, café, shop and
church: check website for opening
times; free (except church); garden:
charge), a massive limestone and
granite neo-Gothic mansion with battlements above its numerous windows,

rears up against a wooded backdrop
on the far side of a reedy lake. It was
built in the 1860s by a wealthy local
MP for his wife, who died tragically
soon after and is commemorated by a
tiny Gothic church. Since the 1920s,
the building has been home to Bene-
dictine nuns, who run it as a girls'
school. The nuns have restored a large
walled Victorian garden, accessible by
mini-bus or forest walk. There's also a
lovely lakeside walk.

Leenane and Killary Harbour

Leenane ❽ (Leenaun on Sat Nav) is
at the inland end of **Killary Harbour**,
Ireland's only fjord. On its southern
shore, **Killary Cruises** (091-566736;
www.killarycruises.com; daily Apr–
Oct) offers one and a half hour harbour
trips and guarantees no seasickness.

In the village, turn left over the
bridge to enjoy the long view down
the harbour (so long that the sea at
its mouth is obscured by mountains),
and visit the **Sheep and Wool Centre**
(tel: 095-42323; www.sheepandwool
centre.com; Apr–Oct daily 9am–6pm;
shop, café: free; museum: charge).
Here, Orla O'Toole, the last big wheel
spinner in Connemara, demonstrates
traditional techniques of spinning,
carding, dyeing and weaving wool, the
main industry in Leenane a hundred
years ago. Some fascinating photos
show the village in those days. Walk
back over the bridge to sample a real
Irish pub, **Hamilton's Bar**, see ①③.

Food & Drink 🍴

③ HAMILTON'S BAR
Leenane; tel: 095-42266; daily
L and AT; €
This old-style pub has a grocery
shop in the front, a pool table in
the back and a pair of petrol
pumps outside, as well as picnic
tables. It serves home-made
soup, open crab or salmon sandwiches and regular sandwiches.

WESTPORT & MAYO

Explore the charms of Westport town, then explore County Mayo with a drive along island-studded Clew Bay to visit Croaghpatrick, Saint Patrick's Holy Mountain. Head inland to the National Museum of Country Life and Foxford Woollen Mills, returning via a scenic hostelry overlooking Lough Cullin.

Mayo is a large county consisting mainly of bog and mountains, with a coastline battered by the Atlantic. It has long been synonymous with remoteness and poverty, but its unspoilt scenery has made it a popular destination for outdoor lovers.

> **DISTANCE** Circular drive: 82km (51 miles)
> **TIME** 1-hour walk; a half-day drive
> **START/END** Westport
> **POINTS TO NOTE**
> Ballina is 16km (10 miles) north of Foxford, and it is 61km (38 miles) from Ballina to Sligo (tour 15).

WESTPORT

Westport ❶ is a compact town of considerable charm, where old Irish ways still prevail. Drive into the centre and park near the highest point. (There is a large car park at the top of Mill Street behind Navin's Funeral Parlour).

The Octagon & Mall

The town was designed in the late 18th century for the Marquess of Sligo to complement his new home, Westport House. All roads lead to the **Octagon**, the town's marketplace. Around its eight sides are some cut-stone Georgian buildings and at its centre is a statue of Saint Patrick on a tall stone plinth.

Walk down James Street; on your left is the **Tourist Information Office** (tel: 098-25711; www.discoverireland.ie/west). Cross the bridge to the **Mall**, a tree-lined thoroughfare that runs beside the canalised Carrowbeg River. Turn right at the next bridge up Bridge Street, which has a landmark **clock tower** at its top. The town has a quirky mix of modern businesses and old traditional ones. Among the latter is a butcher's shop, with an art gallery upstairs and a café, **McCormack's**, see ⓘ①.

Food & Drink

① McCORMACK'S CAFÉ

Bridge Street, Westport; tel: 098-25619; Thur–Sat and Mon B, L and AT; €
Go through the arch and up the stairs to find this café in a cheerful little room. Home-baked cakes, quiches and pâtés are displayed in a cold counter, and there are substantial hot daily specials like bacon and cabbage, or lamb casserole.

Clew Bay & Westport House

Drive from the Octagon down Quay Hill to the **harbour**. The quays face a beautiful stretch of calm water and the island-studded **Clew Bay**. Many of the old warehouses are now hotels and holiday apartments.

From the quays, turn right facing the water and follow the signs for about 200m/yds to reach **Westport House**

Below: sculpture at the Famine Memorial Park, Murrisk.

and Pirates' Adventure Park (tel: 098-27766; www.westporthouse.ie; Apr–Aug daily 11am–6pm; charge). The fine 18th-century house in the classical style has period furniture and paintings, but children prefer the adventure park, with its zoo and swan-shaped pedalos on the lake.

CROAGHPATRICK

The R335 to **Murrisk ❷**, 5km (3 miles) west of Westport, is signposted from the quays. It is a scattered, sea-facing fishing village with two pubs; **The Tavern Bar** is renowned for seafood, see ⑪②.

Beyond Murrisk is the car park for pilgrims who intend to climb to the Holy Mountain, **Croaghpatrick ❸**, known locally as 'The Reek'. Here, the **Croaghpatrick Information Centre** (098-64114; www.croagh-patrick.com) has a café, shop and shower and locker facilities.

The cone-shaped peak is almost 800m (2,600ft) high and has a small oratory. This is where Saint Patrick is said to have rung his bell to summon Ireland's venomous creatures and cast them from the island. On the last Sunday in July about 30,000 people make the ascent, some of them bare-foot. It takes a fit person about three hours there and back, and is well worth the effort for the views of Clew Bay.

Cross the road at the base of Croaghpatrick. Walk beyond a bronze

Food & Drink ⑪

② THE TAVERN BAR
Murrisk; tel: 098-64060; daily L, AT and D; €
Local fishermen used to arrive with buckets of langoustines, starting the bar food tradition here. Fresh seafood is still on offer, but the menu also includes local farmhouse cheeses and locally reared meat. There's a children's menu too.

③ HEALY'S HOTEL
Pontoon; tel: 094-925 6443; www.healyspontoon.com; daily; B, L, AT and D; €–€€
This famous country inn, favoured by fishermen, has turned its lounge bar into a restaurant, such is the demand for its simply prepared seafood, succulent steaks and tasty salads. But what most people remember is the stunning lake view.

sculpture, the centrepiece of the **Famine Memorial Park**; near the shoreline you will find **Murrisk Abbey**, a traditional starting point for the ascent of the Reek. The ruin of an Augustinian friary, founded in 1456, it has some fine stonework in its eastern window.

NORTH OF WESTPORT

Return to Westport and take the N5 east through Castlebar for 24km (16 miles) to Turlough.

National Museum of Country Life

The **National Museum of Country Life ④** (tel: 094-903 1755; www.museum.ie; Tue–Sat 10am–5pm, Sun 2–5pm; free) in Turlough Park houses the National Folklife Collection, illustrating domestic life in rural Ireland from 1850 to about 1950. The displays are hugely appealing to both young and old. The award-winning modern building is in the grounds of a former stately home, and there is a good shop and café here.

Foxford Woollen Mills

Follow the N5 east for about 5km (3 miles) and turn north at Bellavary for another 12km (7 miles) to **Foxford ⑤**. Drive through the village and past the **Admiral Brown Centre** *(see margin)* to find the **Foxford Woollen Mills Visitor Centre** (tel: 094-925 6104; www.museumsofmayo.com; Mon–Sat 10am–6pm, Sun noon–6pm; shop, café and exhibition centre: free; audiovisual

presentation: charge). The mill was founded in 1892 to relieve poverty by a remarkable nun; Foxford is known for high-quality tweeds, rugs and blankets.

Pontoon

Cross the bridge over the River Moy and take the R318 west for 7km (4 miles) to **Pontoon ⑥**. Stop at the car park for a great view of Lough Cullin, surrounded by low hills. Pontoon is not a village as such, but a landbridge dividing Lough Cullin from Lough Conn in the north. Turn left on to the R310 to cross it, enjoying views of water on either side. To bask in the peace and quiet, make a stop at **Healy's**, see ⑪③, a traditional hostelry overlooking the reedy lakeshore.

Return to Castlebar on R310, an almost uninhabited route with thriving birdlife (such as snipe and woodcock), and take the N5 west back to Westport.

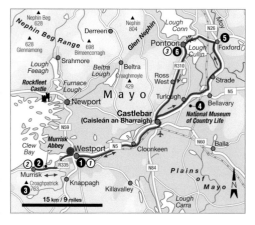

SLIGO & DONEGAL

The counties of Sligo and Donegal are stunningly beautiful. County Sligo has a famous literary heritage, awe-inspiring scenery and fabulous beaches, while County Donegal has a quiet, but breathtaking, magnificence.

Lissadell House

Beautiful 19th-century Lissadell House (www.lissadellhouse.com) was once the home of Yeats's friends the poets Eva and Constance Gore-Booth. Although it is currently closed, a glorious coastal drive takes you past the grounds of the house and back onto the N15 after some 10km (6 miles).

DISTANCE 100km (62miles)
TIME 1 or 2 days
START Sligo town
END Donegal town
POINTS TO NOTE

If you are staying in Sligo town *(see p.114)*, you could return there after visiting Mullaghmore, rather than continuing on to Donegal town. If you are planning to climb Knocknarea, consider an overnight stay.

The best way to Belfast from Donegal is via Omagh and Lisburn. Drive via Derry/Londonderry to visit the Giant's Causeway en route.

County Sligo's dramatically carved coastal scenery is a formidable reminder of the last ice age. This drive takes in some of the county's scenic highlights, including Knocknarea mountain and Lough Gill, as well as the literary highlights of Yeats country, before winding north along the coast towards wind-swept Mullaghmore, the beaches of County Donegal and bustling Donegal town. Linked to the Republic by a slender isthmus, much of Donegal harks back to a remote, rural age. For some here, Irish Gaelic is their first language and, as you head further west into the Gaeltacht area, road signs are written first in Irish and second in English.

SLIGO TOWN

Pretty **Sligo town ❶** is set on the banks of the roaring Garavogue River. Thanks to an enormous rejuvenation project, the town centre is buzzing with shops, cafés and trendy hotels. Sligo hosts an annual W.B. Yeats Summer School, which celebrates its most famous literary export. You can visit a small exhibition on Yeats at the **Sligo County Museum** (Stephen Street; tel: 071-914 2212; www.sligoarts.ie; Tue–Sat 9.30am–12.30pm,

Food & Drink

① **LYONS CAFÉ**
Quay Street, Sligo town; tel: 071-914 2969; Mon–Sat 9am–6pm; €
A Sligo institution since 1923, this spacious department store café is famous for its scones and home-baking. The lunchtime specials are more contemporary.

② **SILVER APPLE**
Lord Edward Street, Sligo town; tel: 071-914 6770; Wed–Sat 5–10pm, Sun 5–10pm and 1–4pm; €€
Modern and friendly, the Silver Apple, above the Gateway pub, serves traditional Irish food with a twist. Try the local sausage and Irish champ or the Lissadell mussels and 'frites'.

May–Sept 2–4.50pm; free). The museum also contains artworks by George Russell, Sean Keating and Yeats's brother Jack B. Yeats. Also worth a visit is the recently renovated **Model Arts and Niland Gallery** (The Mall; tel: 071-914 1405; www.themodel.ie; Wed–Sat 11am–5.30pm, Sun until 5pm; free), with its exhibitions of modern and contemporary Irish and international art. **Lyons Café**, between the town hall and the post office, see ⑪①, is a good option for breakfast; if you plan to return in the evening, try the **Silver Apple** for dinner, see ⑪②.

COASTAL DRIVE

Leaving Sligo town west on the R292, you will arrive, after 5km (3 miles), at the beach resort of **Strandhill ②**. In the daytime, the town attracts families and surfers, thanks to its glorious beach and crashing waves.

For a uniquely relaxing experience, try the **Voya Seaweed Baths** (seafront; tel: 071-916 8686; www.voyaseaweed baths.com; daily 10am–8pm), where you can submerge yourself in a hot bath of seaweed (known for its skin-smoothing properties) or indulge in a hot-stone massage.

Knocknarea & Carrowmore
Signposted off the coast road (R292), southeast of Strandhill, is the starting-point for ascending **Knocknarea ③**, 328m (1,078ft) above sea level. Perched on top of the mountain is an enormous Neolithic tomb (70 by 11m/200 by 35ft), which is said to be the burial place of Queen Mebd (anglicised as 'Maeve'), the warrior queen of Connacht in Celtic mythology. The ascent is steep but worthwhile; the magnificent views suggest why the Celts associated this part of Ireland with myth and magic.

A little further on, just off the R292, is **Carrowmore Megalithic Cemetery ④** (tel: 071-916 1534; Apr–mid-Oct 10am–6pm, last entry 5pm; charge). Ireland's largest megalithic cemetery, it contains 6,000-year-old tombs scattered across the hillsides.

Yeats Country

Although the poet and playwright William Butler Yeats (1865–1939) was actually born in Dublin, his family moved to County Sligo soon after his birth. Yeats would come to regard the county as his ancestral and spiritual home. In 'The Lake Isle of Innisfree' Yeats drew inspiration from a small island on Lough Gill, envisaging a place where he might 'live alone in the bee-loud glade'. In the late poem 'Under Ben Bulben', Yeats included a list of instructions for his burial. He was to be buried in Drumcliff churchyard, nestling under 'bare Ben Bulben's head' (referring to the mountain that dominates the Sligo coastline), and the following epitaph was to be written on his gravestone: *'Cast a cold eye/ On life, on death./ Horseman pass by!'*. Yeats's requests were carried out to the letter.

Yeats's brother Jack B. Yeats (1871–1951) also derived inspiration from the area. Some of his most memorable paintings – often incorporating horse races and scenes of country life – are set in and around the county.

Above from left:
Carrowmore Mega-
lithic Cemetery;
Mullaghmore; Yeats's
grave 'under bare
Ben Bulben's head' at
Drumcliff churchyard.

YEATS COUNTRY

Return to the R292 and continue until it meets the R287 to reach tranquil **Lough Gill ❺**, immortalised by W.B. Yeats in the poem 'The Lake Isle of Innisfree' *(see feature, p.87)*. Rather than driving around the Lough (a detour of some 48km/30 miles), you can stop at a viewing point, signposted just off the R287, by the southwest corner. Return to Sligo via the R287 and R284.

Rosses Point

If you have time, you could make a detour along the R291 (follow the signs, taking a left just past Sligo Harbour) to **Rosses Point**, with its kilometres of beautiful beach, windswept hillside walks and astonishing views both out towards the Atlantic and south towards Knocknarea. The Yeats brothers often spent long, idyllic family holidays at this pleasant spot, wistfully recounted in Yeats's writings.

Drumcliff

About 8km (5 miles) north of Sligo town, on the N15, is the churchyard of **Drumcliff ❻**, Yeats's final resting place. Having died in France in 1939, Yeats was interred here after the Second World War. The spot is delightfully peaceful and Yeats's grave surprisingly unassuming. You can have lunch at the **Drumcliff Tea House and Craft Shop**, while browsing editions of Yeats's poetry, see ⑪③.

MULLAGHMORE TO ROSSNOWLAGH

Signposted off the N15, 12km (7½ miles) north of Drumcliff, is the coast road to **Mullaghmore ❼**, with its vast swathe of golden sand and picture-postcard harbour. The **Pier Head Hotel** here has a snug bar, see ⑪④. Before leaving Mullaghmore, follow the coastal road round to take in windswept **Mullaghmore Head**.

County Donegal Beaches

Leave Mullaghmore by the road that sweeps northeast along the coast to return to the N15. After 8km (5 miles) you will pass into County Donegal (via a small stretch of County Leitrim).

The first resort along the N15 is **Bundoran**, which is trying to shake off its tacky reputation. Bundoran actually marks the point at which County Donegal's 11 Blue Flag beaches begin. Between here and Donegal town, any turn off the main road will take you to one of these beaches; quiet **Rossnowlagh** is particularly recommended.

DONEGAL TOWN

Some 30km (18½ miles) from Bundoran, following the N15 north, is lively **Donegal town ❽**, with its busy triangular 'Diamond' market square. It is a place of contrasts, as Irish-speaking locals encounter tourists in a town that, perhaps surprisingly for its northern position, contains as many familiar high-street cafés and stores as it does craft shops and tearooms. Set on the River Eske, the town is notable for its riverside **castle**, built by the O'Donnell family in the 15th century and redesigned by the Brookes, planters who took over the town in the 17th century. Donegal town is well situated for exploring the dramatic coastline of the northwestern corner of the country. A dinner option in town is **Ard Na Breatha**, see ⑪⑤.

Slieve League

If you have an extra day to spend in Donegal, the astonishingly beautiful cliffs of Slieve League (a transliteration of the Irish Gaelic, Sliabh Liag, meaning 'grey mountain') are a must. They are the highest marine cliffs in Europe, 650m (2,132ft) above sea level at their most easterly point. The cliffs are signposted from the R263 at Carrick (An Charraig). You can drive most of the way to the summit; the walk to the highest point takes in craggy towers, stunning mountain-top pools and hardy sheep. The views out towards the Atlantic, and down onto the cliffs below, are breathtaking, and a little frightening. Another highlight is the sandy beach resort of Naran on the northern side of the peninsula (off the R261).

Food & Drink

③ DRUMCLIFF TEA HOUSE AND CRAFT SHOP
Drumcliff churchyard; tel 071-914 4956; daily 9am–6pm; €
This excellent-value café serves up home-made soups (such as sweet potato and chorizo), stews and salads, and a fabulous selection of scones, cakes and breads.

④ NIMMO'S BAR, PIER HEAD HOTEL
Mullaghmore; tel: 071-916 6171; Sun–Thur 12.30–8.30pm, Fri–Sat 12.30–9pm; €–€€
A traditional pub situated right on Mullaghmore harbour, with outdoor seating. Recently refurbished, it serves pub favourites alongside fish specials, such as crab claws and seafood chowder. The customers are a combination of friendly locals (with their dogs) and tourists. Live music on certain evenings.

⑤ ARD NA BREATHA RESTAURANT
Ard Na Breatha Guest House and Restaurant, Drumrooske, Middle Donegal Town; tel: 074-972 2288; www.ardna breatha.com; daily 7–9.30pm; reservations essential; €€€
Organic, locally sourced seasonal food is served in pleasant, bright surroundings. The three-course set menu is standard, but you can just have one or two courses. The Irish cheeseboard is a must. There's also a snug bar with a roaring fire.

BELFAST

More laid-back than Dublin, with fewer tourists, Belfast exudes a calm confidence. Impressive Victorian architecture, chic bars and restaurants, and quirky museums and libraries mingle in a city that buzzes with possibility.

DISTANCE 2½ miles (4km)
TIME A full day
START Botanic Gardens
END CastleCourt Centre
POINTS TO NOTE

Buses (No 8) run from Queen's Quarter, north to Donegall Square.

Buses (Metro 26 takes 20 minutes) to the Titanic Quarter depart from Wellington Place, on the northwest corner of Donegall Square, and also stop at the Albert Clock Tower. Walkers can follow the Titanic Trail signposts from the City Hall – allow 40 minutes.

If you plan to take a black-taxi tour of west Belfast, it is advisable to book in the morning before you set out. Arrange for the drivers to pick you up somewhere central like Donegall Square.

Belfast is very quiet on Sundays, when shops and city-centre restaurants tend to be open 1–6pm.

Dublin is about 170km (105 miles) south of Belfast via the A1 and M1. Regular trains connect Belfast Central and Dublin's Connolly Station, taking 2–2¼ hours.

Titanic Tours

To explore the history of the RMS *Titanic* and its doomed 1912 voyage you can take a *Titanic* boat tour. Operated by the Lagan Boat Company (tel: 028-9033 0844; www.laganboat company.com; daily at 12.30pm and 2pm; weekends only Nov–Mar; charge), the one-hour tour gives great views of the eerily quiet shipyards, and beautiful Belfast Lough.

Belfast's dominant Victorian and Edwardian architecture resembles more a northern English city, such as Leeds or Liverpool, than the softer Georgian elegance of Dublin. But Northern Ireland's capital has other attributes. A low-rise, open city, framed between lofty green Cave Hill and the great blue bowl of Belfast Lough, it is dotted with lovely parks and open spaces and, for a major city, is surprisingly easy to get around. Above all, it's the people of Belfast who remain its great attraction. Despite preconceptions, they are among the friendliest you will meet, with an easy and down-to-earth sense of humour.

Belfast was the birthplace of the legendary *Titanic*, the most luxurious of liners built in the port's Edwardian heyday. Pride in this legacy is exemplified by the new £97m visitor centre, **Titanic Belfast** in the former dockyards *(see p.92)*. The city offers a centre rich in historical and artistic legacy, with a vibrant bar and restaurant scene.

QUEEN'S QUARTER

Based around Victorian architect Sir Charles Lanyon's distinguished Queen's University, Queen's Quarter is an eclec-

tic mix of elegant wine-bars, scruffy student diners, quirky bookshops and impressive architecture.

Botanic Gardens

Begin the walk at the tranquil **Botanic Gardens ❶** (between College Park and Stranmillis Road; tel: 028-9031 4762; daily 7.30am–dusk; free), laid out in the mid-19th century. Make sure to visit Sir Charles Lanyon's restored curvilinear **Palm House**, and the **Tropical Ravine**, both of which contain exotic flora. Also within the garden is the superb **Ulster Museum** (tel: 028-9044 0000; www.nmni.com/um; Tue–Sun, 10am–5pm; free), whose collection ranges from natural history to contemporary art.

Queen's University

Leave the gardens by the Stranmillis Road exit and walk north along University Road. On the right is the imposing courtyard and red-brick façade of **Queen's University ❷**, which Lanyon based on Magdalen College, Oxford. There are over 100 listed buildings around the campus and surrounding area; to learn more you can visit the **Welcome Centre** (tel: 028-9097 5252; www.qub.ac.uk; Mon–Fri 9.30am–4.30pm, Sat–Sun 11am–4pm; free), which also organises guided tours.

North of Queen's is the atmospheric **Bookfinders Café** (47 University Road; tel: 028-9032 8269), where you can browse the secondhand books with cup of coffee or glass of wine.

Botanic Avenue

Leave University Road by University Square, lined with Victorian terraces, to arrive at College Park, which leads to student-filled **Botanic Avenue**. Look out for shabby-chic **Café Renoir**, a great stop for morning coffee, see ❶①, as well as the excellent crime bookshop **No Alibis** (at no. 83) and retro clothes shops, **The Rusty Zip** (no. 28).

Food & Drink

① CAFÉ RENOIR

95 Botanic Avenue; tel: 028-9031 1300; Sun–Thur 8am–11pm, Fri and Sat 8am–11pm; £

This retro-style café, with a pizzeria attached, is popular with students from Queen's, thanks to its small prices and large portions. There's an excellent choice for breakfast, from pancakes to rib-eye steak, and for lunch, with options such as home-made stews and soups.

Black Cab Taxi Tours

An excellent way of seeing west Belfast – particularly the graphic murals of the (Catholic) Falls and (Protestant) Shankill roads and the peace line built to keep the two areas apart – is by a black-cab tour. Some cab companies are better than others and not all go to the less sanitised Shankill area, where the murals are fresher, and angrier. The tours give an invaluable insight into the political and social reality of the Troubles. A good company is Paddy Campbell's Belfast Black Cab Tours (tel: 028-9061 8479; www.belfastblackcabtours.co.uk). A one-hour tour costs around £30 for 1–3 people (£8.50 each for 4–6 people).

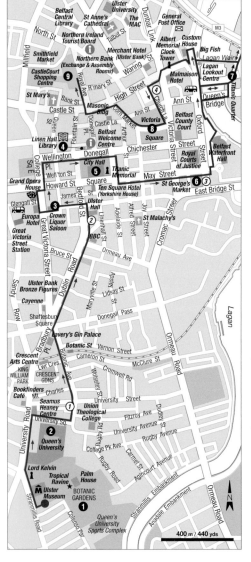

Shaftesbury Square, at the top of Botanic Avenue, was once an integral part of Belfast's 'Golden Mile', established during the Troubles to boost the city's tourism. Celebrity chef Paul Rankin's acclaimed **Cayenne** is here *(see p.121)*. However, the Dublin Road, leading off from the top right-hand corner of Shaftesbury Square, is home to less illustrious – and more affordable – eating-houses.

Ulster Hall

The Dublin Road leads into Bedford Street, home of the distinguished **Ulster Hall** (no. 30; tel: 028-9033 4400; www.belfastcity.gov/uk/ulster hall), a classical gem dating from 1862. It opened as a music hall, and now hosts sporting events, rock gigs, classical music concerts, and beer festivals. An interpretive display tells its history. Next door is **Deane's Deli + Bistro**, a good spot for lunch, see ⑪②.

Great Victoria Street

Turn left beyond the Ulster Hall for Great Victoria Street. On the corner is the glorious **Crown Liquor Saloon** ❸ (no. 46; tel: 028-9024 3187; www. crownbar.com). One of the world's most beautiful Victorian pubs, it was elegantly restored by the National Trust on the advice of the poet John Betjeman. Its 10 wood-panelled snugs,

which were once used by prostitutes, are now fought over by a more salubrious clientele.

Across the road is the **Europa Hotel**, which has the dubious fame of having been the most targeted hotel during the Troubles. Continue north to another ornate building. **The Grand Opera House** (tel: 028-9024 1919; www.goh.co.uk; tours Thur and Sat 11am; charge), topped by white minarets, dates from 1895. Cross the road and turn right (east) into Wellington Place for Donegall Square.

DONEGALL SQUARE

Donegall Square, dominated by the City Hall, is the heart of the city centre. **Belfast Welcome Centre** (47 Donegall Place; tel: 028-9024 6609; www.goto belfast.com; Mon–Sat 9am–5.30pm June–Sept until 7pm, Sun 11am–4pm; free), to the north of the square, is packed full of useful information and has an internet café.

Linen Hall Library

On the northwestern corner of Donegall Square is the quirky **Linen Hall Library** ❹ (no. 17; tel: 028-9032 1707; www.linenhall.com; Mon–Fri 9.30am–5.30pm, Thur until 7pm, Sat 9.30am–4pm; free). Belfast's oldest library, it was founded in 1788 as the Belfast Reading Society and later renamed to reflect the city's linen-producing heritage. Nowadays, it contains an intriguing selection of books and newspapers, comfortable armchairs, internet portals and a small café.

City Hall

The massive **City Hall** ❺ (www.belfastcity.gov.uk; tel:028-9032 0202; Mon–Thur 8.30am–5pm, Fri until 4.30pm; tours Mon–Fri 11am, 2pm and 3pm, Sat 2pm and 3pm), also known as 'the stone Titanic' (the same craftsmen worked on both projects), dominates the square.

Recently renovated, this huge Renaissance Revival-style Edwardian gem, built in 1906, was inspired by London's St Paul's. and has an ornate cathedral-like interior. Even if you don't take a tour, nip in for an eyeful. An exhibition celebrates famous Belfast citizens including George Best, James Galway and Van Morrison. The gardens' are a favourite lunchtime spot in summe and the many monuments here include Thomas Brock's statue of Queen Victoria, and his Titanic Memorial.

Above from far left: Crown Liquor Saloon and Europa Hotel; stained glass window inside City Hall.

Stormont
The grand Parliament Buildings of Stormont, off the Upper Newtownards Road, are home to the rejuvenated Northern Ireland Assembly. Walk around the 100ha (300 acres) of grounds or book a free guided tour (www.niassembly. gov.uk; daily). To get there, take Metro lines 20A or 23 from Queen's Bridge.

Food & Drink
② DEANE'S DELI + BISTRO
44 Bedford Street; tel: 028-9024 8800; Mon–Sat L and D; £–££

Deanes Deli is part of the restaurant empire of innovative Belfast chef Michael Deane. A relaxed café during the day, with fabulous cheese, meat and antipasti boards, it turns into an atmospheric 'vin-café' by night. The delicious food is locally sourced and cooked with a delicate touch. The fish specials – local hake with chorizo, or whole baked monkfish – are a must.

Cathedral Quarter

To the north of the city centre, in the streets surrounding Saint Anne's Cathedral (Donegall Street), a transformation is underway. Fashionable bars and restaurants abound, notably the Great Room at the Merchant Hotel, and the new MAC arts centre firmly establishes the Cathedral Quarter as a rival to Dublin's Temple Bar.

WATERFRONT

Leave Donegall Square in the direction of the waterfront along May Street. After some 250m/yds you will find the neoclassical **Royal Courts of Justice** (1933). Facing them, on the right-hand side of the street, is **St George's Market ⑥** (tel: 028-9043 5704; www.stgeorgesmarket.com; free). Built in 1896 for the sale of fruit, butter, eggs and poultry, it is the oldest market in operation in Ireland. It has hugely popular markets on Fridays, Saturdays and Sundays, selling a host of fresh food and other goods including antiques, crafts and books. The **market stalls** offer an excellent choice for an impromptu lunch or snack, see ⑪③.

LAGANSIDE

Waterfront Hall

After leaving the market, turn left onto Oxford Street and right onto the pedestrianised area by the **Belfast Waterfront Hall** (2 Lanyon Place; tel: 028-9033 4455 for bookings; www.waterfront. co.uk; Mon–Sat from 10am). The glass-fronted galleries, which visitors are free to explore, afford views over Belfast and the River Lagan.

Continuing north along the riverside, pass under Sir Charles Lanyon's 1843 **Queen's Bridge**, and the modern Queen Elizabeth Bridge, to Lagan Weir. The colourful **Big Fish** sculpture has tiles depicting aspects of Belfast's history. This is the embarkation point for the *Titanic Boat Tour (see p.90)*.

At the northern end of Donegall Quay is the elegant mid-19th century **Custom House**, another of Lanyon's architectural achievements.

TITANIC QUARTER

To walk to the **Titanic Quarter ⑦** follow the signposts across the river. The Odyssey (theodyssey.co.uk), is a huge indoor arena used for basketball and rock concerts, which also houses Whowhatwherewhenwhy (W5), a child-friendly interactive discovery centre (w5online.co.uk; tel: 028-9046 7700; charge).

Titanic Belfast (www.titanicbelfast. com; tel: 028-9076 6300; Apr–Sept,

daily 9am–7pm, Sun 10am–5pm; Oct–Mar, daily 10am–5pm; charge) is an unmissable landmark, an architectural extravaganza clad in anodized aluminium, echoing the height and proportions of the gigantic ship's prow. Nine galleries on six storeys give you the tragic story of the ship from her conception to her sinking on 14 April 1912, and its aftermath. **The Titanic Heritage Trail** visits sites nearby associated with the Titanic. The most touching is the Titanic's Dock and Pump House, where the ship stood while being fitted out. Guided walks are available (www.titanicsdock.com; tel: 028-9073 7813; daily on the hour, Mar–Oct 11am–3pm, off season check website; charge).

SHOPPERS' BELFAST

Leaving the riverside area at the Custom House and heading down High Street brings you to the **Albert Memorial Clock Tower**, constructed by Queen Victoria in her husband's memory between 1865 and 1870. It leans 1.25m (4ft) off the vertical, rendering it Belfast's very own 'leaning tower'. About 50m/yds past the Clock Tower, a left turn down Church Lane, home of the excellent café-bar **Muriels**, see ⑪④, will take you to a shopper's paradise.

The newest shopping destination, **Victoria Square** ❽ (tel: 028-9032 2277; www.victoriasquare.com; Mon–Tue 9.30am–7pm, Wed–Fri 9pm, Sat 6pm, Sun 1–6pm) has stores over four levels. The shopping streets of Ann Street, Cornmarket and Castle Street lead to Royal Avenue, home of the older, larger **CastleCourt Centre** ❾ (tel: 028-9023 4591; Mon–Sat 9.30am–7pm, Thur–9pm, Sun 1–6pm).

Above from far left: Albert Memorial Clock Tower; modern Titanic vistors centre building.

Giant's Causeway

If you have a day to spare, the Giant's Causeway, a 2-hour drive north of Belfast (taking the A26), is highly recommended. The existence of the Causeway – an astonishing assembly of more than 40,000 basalt columns, formed into packed hexagonal shapes by the cooling of molten lava – was not even known about until the Bishop of Derry stumbled upon it in 1692. Although the columns are relatively small – the tallest is only about 12m (39ft) high – the sight of them extending further out to sea, in the shadow of craggy red mountains, is breathtaking. Entrance is via the Giant's Causeway Visitor Experience (Causeway Head; tel: 028-2073 1055; www.nationaltrust.org.uk/giants-causeway; daily Jul and Aug 9am–9pm, until 7pm Sept, 5–6pm off season; charge), 2 miles (3km) north of Bushmills on the B146.

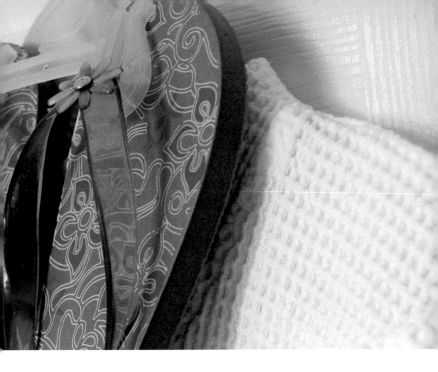

DIRECTORY

A user-friendly alphabetical listing of practical information, plus hand-picked hotels and restaurants, clearly organised by area, to suit all budgets and tastes. Select nightlife listings are also included here.

A

AGE RESTRICTIONS

The age of consent is 17. At 17 you can apply for a driver's licence. The legal drinking age is 18, but some pubs will only serve those over 21 carrying photo ID. You must be 18 to buy cigarettes and tobacco. In the Republic of Ireland under 18s are not allowed on premises that serve alcohol after 9.30pm.

B

BUDGETING

The cost of a pint of draught beer starts from €3.80, and wine from about €4.50 for 175ml. Beer costs approximately €5 a pint in Dublin, and wine about €5.50 a glass, but it could be more in a fashionable bar and up to twice as much in a five-star hotel.

A main course at a budget restaurant costs €10–€15, at a moderate one €18–28 and at an expensive one €28–35.

A double room with breakfast costs about €70–€90 at a B&B or guesthouse, €90–€120 at a moderate hotel and €160–€220 at an expensive hotel.

A taxi from Dublin airport to the city centre costs about €25. A single bus ticket in Dublin or Cork costs €1.60, and a Dublin tram (Luas) ticket costs €1.50 for a similar distance. A one-day travel card for both bus and tram in Dublin costs €7.50.

Admission to national museums in both the Republic and Northern Ireland is free. Charges for other heritage attractions vary from €3–€12 and up. A Heritage Card (adult: €21, family: €55) gives free admission to over 90 national sights and monuments (www.heritage ireland.ie). Heritage Island offers up to €500 worth of discounts at over 95 locations for two people travelling together, if you buy a copy of their guide (€6.99; www.heritageisland.com). From Dublin Tourism, you can buy a pass that gives free admission to 30 sights plus other concessions (for one day, adult: €35, child: €19; www.dublinpass.ie).

C

CHILDREN

Irish people love children. They are usually welcome at hotels and B&Bs, most of which can supply special cots or babysitting services. Many hotels allow children to stay in their parents' room at no extra charge; check when booking. Some of the grander country houses will only accept children over 12.

Most restaurants can supply highchairs and a children's menu; bigger restaurants and pubs should have nappy-changing facilities. Kids are generally welcome in pubs up to about 7pm (and by law under 18s must be gone by 9.30pm), but this is at the discretion of the landlord, and children should be supervised by an adult at all times.

During holiday periods, there are plenty of child-oriented activities organised by museums, local festivals and outdoor centres; tourist offices *(see p.105)* will have full details.

CLOTHING

You can safely leave your formal clothes at home, unless you are going to the Wexford Festival Opera. Smart-casual is acceptable just about everywhere. Because of the unpredictability of the weather, pack an umbrella, some rain-proof clothing and a warm sweater, even in summer. But bring the suntan cream as well; it does shine sometimes.

For climate information, *see p.12.*

CRIME & SAFETY

While rural Ireland is a low-risk area for crime, hired cars are easy targets for criminals, and thefts from cars are commonplace in Dublin, other major towns and cities, and in the car parks of visitor attractions. Never leave anything visible in your car, even if you are only leaving it briefly. Be careful when withdrawing money from ATMs, and shield your pin number. Beware of pickpockets in crowded places. In central Dublin ask your hotel whether it is safe to walk home in the dark (take particular care around the Lower Gardiner Street and Connolly Station). It is sensible to keep a copy of your passport in case of theft.

Victims of crime in the Republic should contact Irish Tourist Assistance Service, Garda HQ, Harcourt Square, Dublin 2; tel: 01-666 6666; www.itas.ie.

For emergencies, *see p.100.*

CUSTOMS

Visitors of all nationalities entering or leaving the EU via Ireland or Northern Ireland must declare on arrival or departure sums of cash above €10,000.

Visitors within the EU may import the following goods, provided they were purchased within the EU and are for personal use: 800 cigarettes, 400 cigarillos, 200 cigars, 1kg tobacco, 10 litres spirits, 20 litres fortified wines, 90 litres wine, 110 litres beer.

From outside the EU you may import duty-free: 200 cigarettes or the tobacco equivalent, 4 litres of wine or 1 litre of spirits, and other goods to the value of €430 per person.

For details of restricted goods, see www.revenue.ie.

Non-EU visitors can claim back sales taxes on purchases made in the Republic. Participating stores have a 'Tax Free Shopping' sign in the window. You must complete a tax refund document, and present this and the goods to customs on departure. Some airports will refund you on the spot; otherwise, mail the validated document back to the store and a refund will be issued. The VAT rate on most items is 23 percent.

Above from far left: playing by St Patrick's in Dublin; Ha'Penny Bridge across the Liffey; looking out over the Cliffs of Moher.

Etiquette

The Irish love to talk, and they expect visitors to respond in kind. Do not wait to be introduced; strike up a conversation with the person sitting next to you at the bar or on the bus, and be prepared to tell your life story. In Ireland it is perfectly acceptable to talk to strangers; no one will think you are mad, as they might do in big European cities. Pub etiquette is based on good manners: if somebody buys you a drink, buy one back; if a group includes you in the drinks order (a 'round'), offer to buy the next one. Avoid being drawn into discussions of politics or religion while alcohol is being consumed. Avoid telling people what's wrong with their country (eg the roads, the sign-posts, the high cost of everything); they know already.

D

DISABLED TRAVELLERS

Ireland is still introducing facilities such as ramps and accessible toilets for people with disabilities. Public transport lags behind, especially outside Dublin. However, visitors with disabilities often find that people's helpfulness makes up for the lack of amenities.

In the Republic, the key organisation for practical information, wheelchair rental and parking permits is the Irish Wheelchair Association (Áras Chú-chulainn, Blackheath Drive, Clontarf, Dublin; tel: 01-818 6400; www.iwa.ie). The official government body is the National Disability Authority (25 Clyde Road, Ballsbridge, Dublin 4; tel: 01-608 0400; www.nda.ie). The Head Office of Fáilte Ireland *(see p.104)* can advise on attractions and accommodation suitable for disabled visitors.

In Northern Ireland, Disability Action (2 Annadale Ave, Belfast; tel: 028-9029 7880; www.disabilityaction. org) offers practical advice.

E

ELECTRICITY

220 volts AC (50 cycles) is standard. Hotels usually have dual 220/110 voltage sockets for electric razors only. Most sockets require a 3-pin plug; visitors may need an adaptor.

EMBASSIES & CONSULATES

Dublin

Australia. Fitzwilton House, Wilton Terrace, Dublin 2; tel: 01-664 5300; www.ireland.embassy.gov.au.

Britain. 29 Merrion Road, Dublin 4; tel: 01-205 3700; www.britishembassy inireland.fco.gov.uk.

Canada. 7–8 Wilton Terrace, Dublin 2; tel: 01-234 4000; www.canada.ie.

US. 42 Elgin Road, Dublin 4; tel: 01-668 8777; http://dublin.usembassy.gov.

Belfast

American Consulate General. Danesfort House, 223 Stranmillis Road, Belfast BT9 5GR; tel: 028-9038 6100; http://belfast.usconsulate.gov

EMERGENCIES

In an emergency, dial 999; 112 is also used in the Republic.

G

GAY/LESBIAN ISSUES

There should be no major problems for gay and lesbian travellers in Ireland. Be as safety conscious as you would in any foreign city or country. Openly gay couples may attract unwanted attention in small-town pubs.

Information on LGBT-friendly bars and clubs, accommodation and advice

and contacts can be found through the following organisations:

Dublin. Outhouse, 51 Capel Street; tel: 01-873 4933; www.outhouse.ie; and Gay Switchboard, tel: 01-872 1055; www.gayswitchboard.ie.

Cork. The Other Place, South Main Street; tel: 021-427 8470; www.the otherplacecork.com.

West of the Shannon. Out West Ireland, PO Box 58, Castlebar, County Mayo; tel: 087-972 5586; www.out westireland.ie.

Belfast. Queer Space, Old War Memorial Building, 9–13 Waring Street, BT12DX; www.queerspace.org.uk.

GREEN ISSUES

Ireland has an active Green Party, but green issues and sustainable planning are minority concerns. Recycling is in its infancy, and much waste still goes to landfill; however, a small charge for plastic bags in supermarkets has been effective. Solar energy and wind power are also nascent, although there are controversial plans for giant wind farms in the west. Many of Ireland's smaller farms are now managed under REPs (Rural Environment Protection Scheme), to encourage wildlife and biological diversity. But overuse of fertilizer in farming and forestry has led to pollution of lakes and rivers.

For the latest, visit www.friendsofthe irishenvironment.org. For carbon-offsetting your trip, *see margin, right*.

H

HEALTH

Medical insurance is advisable for all visitors. However, visitors from EU countries are entitled to medical treatment in the Republic and Northern Ireland under reciprocal arrangements.

With the exception of UK citizens, visitors from EU states should obtain the European Health Insurance Card, which entitles the holder to free treatment by a doctor and free medicines on prescription. If hospital treatment is necessary, this will be given free in a public ward. UK visitors need only go to a doctor (or, in an emergency, a hospital), present some proof of identity (eg a driving licence) and request treatment under the EU health agreement.

Hospitals and Pharmacies

Dublin. St Vincent's University Hospital, Merrion Road, Dublin 4; tel: 01-221 4000; www.stvincents.ie.

Hamilton Long pharmacy, 5 Lower O'Connell Street; tel: 01-874 8456.

Belfast. Belfast City Hospital, 51 Lisburn Road; tel: 028-9032 9241.

Urban Pharmacy, 56 Dublin Road, BT2 7HN; tel: 028-9024 6336.

HOURS & HOLIDAYS

Shops and department stores usually open Mon–Sat 9.30am–5.30 or 6pm. In smaller towns some shops close for

Carbon-Offsetting
Air travel produces a huge amount of carbon dioxide and is a significant contributor to global warming. If you would like to offset the damage caused to the environment by your flight, a number of organisations can do this for you using online 'carbon calculators' that tell you how much you need to donate. In the UK travellers can visit www.climatecare. org or www.carbon neutral.com; in the US log on to www. climatefriendly.com or www.sustainable travelinterational.org.

lunch between 1pm and 2pm. Supermarkets and convenience stores generally open daily until 9pm. Post offices open Mon–Fri 9am–5.30pm and Sat 9am–1pm. Government offices are open Mon–Fri 9am–5pm.

Museums and other tourist sights are often closed on Monday, and outside Dublin and Belfast most have restricted opening hours between November and Easter or late May.

In hotels and B&Bs, breakfast is generally served from 8–10am, and in restaurants and pubs until noon. Restaurants and pubs generally serve lunch between 12.30 and 2.30pm, and dinner from 6 to 9.30pm.

Public Holidays

1 Jan: New Year's Day
17 Mar: St Patrick's Day
Mar/Apr: Good Fri and Easter Mon
1st Mon May: May Day
Last Mon May: Bank Holiday (NI)
1st Mon June: Bank Holiday (RoI)
12 July: Bank Holiday (NI)
1st Mon Aug: Bank Holiday (RoI)
Last Mon Aug: Bank Holiday (NI)
Last Mon Oct: Bank Holiday (RoI)
25 Dec: Christmas Day
26 Dec: Boxing Day

I

INTERNET FACILITIES

Wi-fi is widely available free in cafés, bars and public areas of hotels. Most hotels also have a computer available for public access; if yours does not, ask for directions to the nearest internet café.

M

MAPS

Cyclists and walkers may want small-scale maps; these can be bought locally from bookshops, newsagents and tourist offices. The latter usually also offer a free town and surrounding area map.

MEDIA

Print Media. *The Irish Times* is Ireland's newspaper of record, with good coverage of foreign news, arts and business. The *Irish Independent* is published daily in Dublin, and the *Irish Examiner* in Cork. Two morning papers are published in Belfast, the *Belfast Newsletter* and *Irish News*. Each city also publishes an evening paper, useful for entertainment listings.

Television and Radio. In the Republic RTÉ (www.rte.ie) broadcasts three channels including Irish-language TG4 (www.tg4.ie). Most UK channels are available on satellite or cable TV, which is widespread in hotels and B&Bs (confirm on booking). In Northern Ireland, the BBC1 (www.bbc.co.uk) includes local coverage, as does its commercial counterpart, UTV (www.u.tv).

In the Republic RTÉ1 is the main radio station for news, current affairs

and drama, 2FM plays pop music and Lyric FM is for lovers of classical music. There are also a number of independent local radio stations. In Northern Ireland the commercials-free BBC Radio Ulster has full local coverage, as do Downtown Radio (MW) and Cool FM.

MONEY

Currency. The Republic of Ireland is in the Eurozone. Banknotes come in denominations of €5, €10, €20, €50, €100, €200 and €500, coins in denominations of 1, 2, 5, 10, 20 and 50 cents, €1 and €2. In Northern Ireland, the British pound (£) is the standard currency, although most traders in border areas are prepared to accept euros. Banknotes: £5, £10, £20 and £50; coins: 1p, 2p, 5p, 10p, 20p, 50p, £1 and £2.

Banking Hours. Banks are open Mon–Fri 10am–4pm, with one day late opening until 5pm (Thur in Dublin). Smaller town banks may close for lunch from 12.30–1.30pm.

Cash Machines. Nearly all banks have 24-hour cash machines (ATMs), but not all towns have banks. In smaller places, cash machines can be found in convenience stores. Check with your bank before leaving home to confirm that your bankcard will work in Ireland.

Credit Cards. The most widely accepted cards are Visa and Mastercard, followed by American Express. Many but not all guest houses and B&Bs take credit cards; check in advance.

Traveller's Cheques. This is one of the safest ways of carrying money, but these days they are rarely used outside of banks. If lost or stolen, cheques can be replaced, usually within 24 hours in the case of American Express.

Tipping. Tipping is not expected in bars, except in lounge bars where drinks are brought to your table. It is usual to give at least a 10 percent tip to waiting staff. Round taxi fares to the nearest euro or pound, and porters are given about €1 or £1 a bag.

P

POLICE

The Republic is policed by the Garda Síochána (Guardians of the Peace), and Northern Ireland by the Police Service of Northern Ireland (PSNI). In an emergency, dial 999; 112 is also used in the Republic.

POST

Postage stamps are sold by post offces, newsagents and general stores. Letters and postcards cost 55 cents to send within the Republic and 82 cents to the UK, mainland Europe and North America; they cost 60p within the UK, 87p to Europe and £1.28p to the rest of the world. In the Republic most letterboxes are pillar-shaped and are painted green; in Northern Ireland the letterboxes are red. Note that Republic

Above from far left: Dublin bus tours; letter box with the modern Irish Gaelic name for Dublin.

Religion

The free practice of religion is guaranteed by the constitution in the Republic, and there is no state religion. However, most of the population belongs to Christian denominations, predominantly Catholicism. The second largest congregation is the Episcopalian-affiliated Church of Ireland. Islam, consisting mostly of recent Muslim emigrants, is now the third largest congregation (see www.islamireland.ie). While church attendance on Sundays by Catholics has dropped off in Dublin, it remains a strong tradition in rural Ireland. About two-thirds of the population of Northern Ireland is Protestant, with Catholics generally living in specific areas.

of Ireland stamps may not be used on mail posted in Northern Ireland and vice versa.

Post Offices. Hours are generally Mon–Fri 9am–5.30pm and Sat 9am–1pm. The General Post Offices in the two capitals are at O'Connell Street, Dublin (tel: 01-705 7000) and 25 Castle Place, Belfast (tel: 028-9024 9237).

S

SMOKING

Smoking is banned in all workplaces, including taxis, bars, restaurants and nightclubs. Elaborate sheltered outdoor smoking areas are provided by many pubs and clubs.

T

TELEPHONES

The international dialling code for the Republic of Ireland is 353. Northern Ireland's is 44. If you are calling the North from the Republic, just substitute the code 028 with 048, rather than using the international dialling code.

There are several telecommunications companies operating in Ireland, the largest one being Eircom (www.eircom.ie). Public telephones mainly use phone cards, which are widely available from newsagents and supermarkets. Phone boxes are gradually disappearing, as the mobile phone gains dominance. Inter-

national calls can be dialled direct from private phones, or dial 1901 for customer service. For directory enquiries dial 11811, for international directory enquiries 11818. The long-distance services of BT Ireland, AT&T, Sprint and MCI are also available.

Services in Northern Ireland are operated by British Telecom (www.bt.com); dial 100 for the operator.

Mobile (Cell) Phones. Only mobiles with GSM will work in Ireland. If your phone is non-GSM, consult with your provider before travelling. It may be cheaper to buy a local SIM card and top up with prepaid calls. Local providers include 3, Meteor, 02, Tescomobile and Vodafone. If you are coming from the UK, your mobile should work in Northern Ireland, but you will need international roaming in the Republic.

TIME ZONES

Ireland follows Greenwich Mean Time. In spring, the clock moves one hour ahead for Summer Time; in autumn it moves back to GMT. At noon – according to GMT – it is 4am in Los Angeles, 7am in New York, 1pm in western Europe, 8pm in Singapore, 10pm in Sydney and midnight in New Zealand.

TOURIST INFORMATION

Fáilte Ireland Dublin Head Office. Tel: 0808 234 2009; www.discoverireland.ie. For tourist information, tel:

1850 230 330 in Ireland, tel: 0800 039 7000 in the UK).

Dublin Tourism Centre. Suffolk Street (near Grafton Street); tel: 01-605 7700; www.visitdublin.com.

Regional Offices. Local tourist offices can be found throughout Ireland. A number are mentioned in the tours in this guide; otherwise, for details see www.discoverireland.ie.

Northern Ireland Tourist Board. 59 North Street, Belfast BT1 1NB; tel: 028-9023 1221; www.discovernorthern ireland.com.

TRANSPORT

Arrival by Air

There are flights from Britain and Europe to Belfast, Dublin, Cork and Shannon airports, with over 30 airlines flying from 70 destinations. There are also frequent flights from British airports to regional airports in Kerry, Galway, Waterford and Knock (County Mayo).

The main carriers from Britain are Aer Arann (www.aerarann.com), Aer Lingus (www.aerlingus.com), bmi (www.flybmi.com), bmibaby (www. bmibaby.com), easyJet (www.easyjet. com) and Ryanair (www.ryanair.com).

There are direct flights from the US to both Dublin and Shannon airports and Belfast International Airport. The main carriers are Aer Lingus (www.aer lingus.com), American Airlines (www. aa.com), Continental Airlines (www. continental.com), Delta Airlines (www. delta.com) and US Airways (www. usairways.com).

Airport to City

Republic. There is a regular bus service from **Dublin Airport** (tel: 01-814 1111; www.dublinairport.com) to the main bus station in the city centre (30 min), while Aircoach (www.air coach.ie) departs every 10–20 minutes for various city locations. The bus from **Cork Airport** (tel: 021-431 3131; www.corkairport.com) to the city takes about 10 minutes. From **Shannon Airport** (tel: 061-471444; www.shannonairport.com) there is a regular bus service to Limerick city (30 min).

A **taxi** from the airport to the city centre should cost approximately €25 in Dublin, €10 in Cork and €35 in Shannon (to Limerick).

Northern Ireland. There are two major airports: **Belfast International**, (tel: 028-9448 4848; www.belfastairport. com) a 30-minute bus ride from town or about £27 by taxi, and **George Best Airport** (tel: 028-9093 9093; www.bel fastcityairport.com), a short bus or taxi ride from the town centre. For more information on access to and from airports see www.discoverireland.com.

Arrival by Sea

Ireland has six main ferry ports; Republic: Cork, Dublin, Dun Laoghaire (12km/7½ miles south of Dublin) and

Above from far left: cycling in Wicklow; walking to the beach at Lahinch, County Clare.

Toilets
Public toilets are usually available in a town's main car park, at tourist offices and at big petrol stations. Most large supermarkets and all department stores have public toilets. Most pubs reserve their toilets for their customers' use only; a hotel is a better bet.

Above: Dublin cabs.

Rosslare (County Wexford); Nothern Ireland: Belfast and Larne (County Antrim). For details of operators and routes, see www.discoverireland.com.

Public Transport in Ireland

Outside Dublin, public transport is limited. **Bus Éireann** (01-836 6111, www.buseireann.ie) serves provincial Ireland with both local and direct express services. Its Expressway timetable (€3) is essential if you plan to travel by bus, and its Open Road passes allow flexible cross-country travel. Dublin's main bus station (Busáras) is on Store Street.

Iarnród Éireann (Irish Rail; 01-836 6222, www.irishrail.ie) runs rail services from Connolly, Pearse Street and Heuston stations to the main towns in Ireland, including Belfast. Fares are reasonable (eg Dublin–Cork return: €74, Dublin–Galway return: €52). Irish Rail also has a limited number of cut-price tickets available online.

The Republic is one of 21 countries in which you can use the global Eurail-pass (www.eurail.com).

For details on public transport by bus and rail in Northern Ireland (and the Metro in Belfast), call 028-9066 6630 or visit www.translink.co.uk.

Public Transport In Dublin

Dublin Bus (tel: 01-873 4222; www. dublinbus.ie) has an extensive network within the greater Dublin area, with priority bus lanes ensuring progress through the often gridlocked traffic. Dublin Bus requires exact change to be given, and will not accept notes.

The bus network is supplemented by the **Luas** tram system (tel: 01-800 300604 within Republic; www.luas.ie). Purchase of a one- or three-day travel card, widely available from newsagents, will give best value. For ticket costs, *see budgeting, p.98.*

The **DART** (www.irishrail.ie), a rapid transit railway, runs from the city centre along the coast from Howth in the north to Greystones in the south.

Taxis

There are metered taxis in Belfast, Cork, Dublin, Galway and Limerick. In other areas, fares should be agreed beforehand. Taxis are usually found at ranks in central locations, or booked by phone, and do not usually cruise the streets. **Global Taxis** (tel 01-872 7272; www.globaltaxis.ie) is one of the biggest Dublin companies.

Driving

Outside the cities, Irish roads are still among the least congested in Europe, although it is hard to believe this when you are stuck in a traffic jam in Dublin's ever-expanding suburbs.

Rules of the Road. Drive on the left on both sides of the border. All passengers must wear seat belts. Drink driving laws are strict, and it is an offence to drive with a concentration of alcohol exceeding 50mg per 100ml of blood.

Remember that in the Republic speed limit signs are in kilometres. The limit is 50km/h (31mph) in urban areas, 80km/h (50mph) on non-national roads, 100km/h (62mph) on national routes (green signposts) and 120km/h (75mph) on motorways. On-the-spot fines can be issued for speeding offences.

In Northern Ireland, the limit in urban areas is 30mph (48km/h), on country roads 60mph (96km/h), and 70mph (113km/h) on motorways and dual-carriageway trunk roads.

Tolls. There are toll charges for using the M50 Dublin orbital motorway and the M1 northern motorway, the Dublin Port tunnel, Limerick tunnel, the Waterford bypass and some sections of rural motorway. Visit www.eflow.ie for information on barrier-free tolling.

Car Hire. Be sure to book in advance for July and August. Car hire is expensive in Ireland, and advance booking as part of a fly-drive or train-ferry-drive package often leads to a better deal, as does booking online. Drivers under 25 and over 70 may have to pay a higher rate. Most companies will not rent cars to people over 76. If you intend to drive across the border, inform your rental company beforehand to check that you are fully insured.

Local and international car hire companies in both the Republic and Northern Ireland are listed on www.carhireireland.com.

V

VISAS & PASSPORTS

UK citizens do not require a passport to enter Ireland, but most carriers by air or sea ask for photographic ID, usually either a passport or driving licence. Check with the individual company before travelling.

Non-UK nationals must have a valid passport. EU nationals and travellers from the US, Canada, Australia, New Zealand and South Africa are simply required to show a passport. Visitors of all other nationalities should contact their local Irish embassy or consulate before travelling to the Republic, or their British Embassy, High Commission or Consular Office before travelling to Northern Ireland.

W

WEBSITES

www.discoverireland.com – the official website of Failte Ireland, covering the Republic and Northern Ireland
www.discovernorthernireland.com – detailed information on the North
www.entertainment.ie – for theatre, cinema, club and festival listings
www.gulliver.ie – accommodation reservation network of Failte Ireland
www.hostels-ireland.com – Tourist Board-approved holiday hostels
www.met.ie – for the latest forecast

Weights and Measures
The metric system has been adopted in the Republic and Northern Ireland, but is not always enforced. For example, beer comes in pints, petrol comes in litres, while food is sold in both pounds and kilograms.

At the top end of Ireland's hotels offerings are the grand city landmarks, elegant castles and country houses. The middle range includes new hotels with elaborate spa facilities and lovingly converted period buildings. The inexpensive hotels tend to be family-owned or guest houses (just like a hotel, but with no bar or restaurant). Most B&Bs come into the economy category, but even so you can expect a bathroom en suite and a good standard of comfort.

Book in advance June–Sept and for Dublin year round. If you are staying for more than one night, ask for a reduced rate. Book either directly with the hotel or through www.discoverireland.com, which also lists self-catering options.

Dublin

Aberdeen Lodge

55 Park Avenue; tel: 01-283 8155; www.aberdeen-lodge.com; €€€
A large three-storey Victorian house in the elegant south Dublin area of Ballsbridge, with really spacious bedrooms, all beautifully furnished. Regular buses run to the city centre, and it is also close to Sydney Parade DART station.

Price for a double room for one night with breakfast:

€€€€€	over 200 euros
€€€€	160–200 euros
€€€	120–160 euros
€€	90–120 euros
€	under 90 euros

Bewley's Hotel Ballsbridge

Merrion Road; tel: 01-668 1111; www.bewleyshotels.com/ballsbridge; €€
A large, excellent-value hotel next to the RDS Arena, in a converted 19th-century Masonic building. Over 300 rooms are offered at a flat per-room rate, with fresh Bewley's coffee and free wi-fi as standard. There is also a lively lounge bar and a good restaurant.

Central Hotel

2 Exchequer Street; www.central hoteldublin.com; €€€
Close to both Grafton Street and Temple Bar, this rambling Victorian hotel has an excellent location, and a mildly Bohemian atmosphere. Its cosy first floor Library Bar is a haunt of literary types.

Charles Stewart Parnell Guest House

5–6 Parnell Square; tel: 01-878 0350; www.charlesstewart.ie; €–€€
This lovely Georgian house is right on Parnell Square, near a bus stop to the airport. The rooms have simple decor and are well maintained; the young staff are helpful and enthusiastic. Excellent value.

Harcourt Hotel

60 Harcourt Street; tel: 01-478 3677; www.harcourthotel.ie; €–€€
Harcourt occupies a row of Georgian houses, just off St Stephen's Green.

Rooms are small, and can be noisy as the hotel has a nightclub, but the location and ambience make it good value nevertheless.

The Merrion

Upper Merrion Street; tel: 01-603 0600; www.merrionhotel.com; €€€€€

A stunning hotel, converted from four Georgian townhouses, with individually designed rooms and suites, each with beautiful bathrooms. So discreet it even lacks a hotel sign, using instead a small, traditional Georgian brass plaque.

Number 31

31 Lesson Close; tel: 01-676 5011; www.number31.ie; €€€€

Combining a classic Georgian townhouse with a Modernist mews, this beautiful hotel is situated close to Fitzwilliam Square. Famous for its excellent breakfasts and unique 'sunken lounge'.

O'Callaghan Davenport

Merrion Square; tel: 01-607 3700; www.ocallaghanhotels.com; €€€

This elegant four-star hotel is well sited for the city centre, Merrion Square and Trinity College. Rooms are large, comfortable and surprisingly good value.

Hotel St George

7 Parnell Square; tel: 01-874 5611; www.thecastlehotelgroup.com; €€

A large townhouse, nicely decorated in the Georgian style, with the occasional antique. It has a real 'old Dublin' feel, even though it is right in the middle of everything. Ask for an interior room overlooking the garden if you like quiet.

The Westbury Hotel

Grafton Street; tel: 01-679 1122; www.doylecollection.com; €€€€–€€€€€

Consistently rated one of the most popular hotels in Dublin, the Westbury Hotel prides itself on its level of luxury, its city centre location and its excellent restaurant. Book online for large savings.

Around Dublin: County Wicklow

Sheepwalk House and Cottages

Avoca; tel: 0402-35189; www. sheepwalk.com; €

A lovely guesthouse, with self-catering cottages for a longer stay, just 2km (1¼ miles) outside Avoca. Check out the individually decorated rooms on the website before you book.

Woodenbridge Hotel

Vale of Avoca, Arklow (on the R752); tel: 0402-35146; www.woodenbridge hotel.com; €

Although it has seen better days, this hotel is a bargain for County Wicklow, with bright, spacious rooms, a decent breakfast and lovely views over the Vale of Avoca.

Above from far left: O'Callaghan Davenport hotel.

Youth Hostels
The Irish Youth Hostel Association, An Óige, has a comprehensive website (www. anoige.ie) with an excellent choice of hostels throughout the Republic. For hostels in Northern Ireland, Hostelling International NI (www.hini.org.uk) has hostels in Belfast and on the Causeway coast.

Southeast: Kilkenny

Butler House

16 Patrick Street, Kilkenny city; tel: 056-776 5707; www.butler.ie; €€

Once the Dower House of Kilkenny Castle, the reception rooms here have ornate plaster ceilings and marble fireplaces, while the bedrooms have clean-lined modern decor. Breakfast is served in the Design Centre, a short walk across the garden. There's no bar or restaurant, but you are right in the centre of town. Book well in advance.

Mount Juliet Conrad

Thomastown, County Kilkenny; tel: 056-777 3000; www.mountjuliet. ie; €€€–€€€€€

This elegant 18th-century house is the centrepiece of a 600ha (1,500-acre) estate by the River Nore, which includes a Jack Nicklaus-designed golf course, equestrian centre, tennis centre and luxury spa. Rooms in the main house have impeccable period decor plus modern facilities, albeit at a price. There are smaller, more affordable rooms in the Hunter's Yard, and a less formal restaurant called Kendal's.

Price for a double room for one night with breakfast:

€€€€€	over 200 euros
€€€€	160–200 euros
€€€	120–160 euros
€€	90–120 euros
€	under 90 euros

Southeast: Waterford & Cashel

Cashel Palace Hotel

Main Street, Cashel; tel: 062-62707; www.cashel-palace.ie; €€€€–€€€€€

The Bishop of Cashel's palace is now a luxury hotel surrounded by gardens. Its back bedrooms overlook the Rock of Cashel, which is connected to it by a footpath. Rooms are both luxurious and characterful, including the newly converted ones in the mews.

Granville Hotel

The Quay, Waterford city; tel: 051-305555; www.granville-hotel.ie; €€

The Granville's porticoed entrance has been a landmark on Waterford's quays for generations. The hotel has retained its Georgian character through many refurbishments, but remains likeably old fashioned. It is perfectly located for exploring the city on foot.

Southwest: Cork City & Environs

Ballymaloe House

Shanagarry, Midleton; tel: 021-465 2531; www.ballymaloe.ie; €€€€€

One of Ireland's leading country house hotels, Ballymaloe is tastefully decorated and has high standards. The kitchen is renowned for its pioneering use of fresh local produce, including home-grown vegetables and soft fruit from the hotel's own farm. It is less than an hour's drive east of Cork city off the N25.

Clarion Hotel

Lapp's Quay, Cork; tel: 021-422 4900; www.clarionhotelcorkcity.com; €€

A large hotel in the centre of town by the River Lee, the Clarion is a pioneer of the proposed docklands development. There's a central atrium with a wide staircase, which some bedrooms overlook; if you want an exterior view, say so. Bedrooms have chic, minimalist decor, while the bar extends on to a riverside walk and is a popular early evening spot.

Gabriel House

Summerhill North, St Luke's Cross, Cork; tel: 021-450 0333; www.gabriel-house.ie; €

This large detached building was previously a Christian Brothers seminary, but makes a characterful budget hotel. It's on a bluff high above the railway station, a five minute uphill walk from the centre; the best and largest rooms have a river view. Nearby Henchy's is a gem of a Victorian pub.

Southwest: West Cork

Rolf's Country House

Baltimore Hill, Baltimore; tel: 028-20289; www.rolfscountryhouse.eu; €€€€

A converted old stone-built farmhouse and outbuildings on a site high above Roaring Water Bay. Bedrooms are small and simple, with white cotton bedlinen and casement windows. The café and restaurant are pleasantly informal, with exhibitions by local artists. The village is about a mile away and has a lively pub and café scene in summer.

Trident Hotel

Kinsale; tel: 021-477 9300; www.tridenthotel.com; €€

Watch the boats come and go from this modern waterside hotel, adjacent to the town pier, where all rooms have sea views. The Wharf Bar is popular with locals for bar food.

Southwest: Ring of Kerry

Carrig Country House

Caragh Lake, Glenbeigh; tel: 066-976 9100; www.carrighouse.com; €€€

You can hear the waters of the lake lapping from your bedroom in this magical hideaway. The Victorian manor house is set in carefully tended lakeside gardens, with views of the wild mountains. Bedrooms are furnished in Victorian style with antique furniture; the peaceful sitting room is lined with books; and the restaurant is excellent.

Loch Lein Country House Hotel

Fossa, Killarney; tel: 064-663 1260; www.lochlein.com; €€€

Situated 4km (2½ miles) outside Killarney just off the main Ring of Kerry (N72), this new traditional-style 25-room hotel makes an excellent touring base. It occupies a secluded location with tantalising views of Loch Lein across the fields.

Parknasilla Resort

Sneem; tel: 064-667 5600;
www.parknasillahotel.ie; €€€€

Set amid 200ha (500 acres) of balmy sub-tropical vegetation on a sheltered sea inlet, with a dramatic backdrop of mountains, this is one of Ireland's most famous resort hotels. Opt for a room in the main house or the cheaper self-catering houses (sleeping six). The bedrooms have been fully upgraded as has the pool and spa, while the lounge and bar retain a mildly eccentric old-fashioned charm.

Ballygarry House Hotel and Spa

Killarney Road, Tralee; tel: 066-712 3322; www.ballygarryhouse.com; €€€

This family-run country house-style hotel has been extended without losing the quiet charm of the original. A mile and a half outside town, it is a great touring base, with mountain views, and forest walking trails on the doorstep. The bar has a large local clientele, and the restaurant is a favourite for special occasions, while residents can enjoy their own drawing room and library. The spa is excellent.

Greenmount House

Upper John Street, Dingle; tel: 066-915 1414; www.greenmounthouse.ie; €€–€€€

Although only a short walk from the town centre, this quiet 14-room guesthouse is surrounded by country fields and has a lovely view of the sun setting over Dingle Harbour. Rooms are spacious, with uncluttered contemporary decor. The home-baking and breakfast here are renowned.

Dromoland Castle

Newmarket-on-Fergus,
County Clare; tel: 061-368144;
www.dromoland.ie. €€€€€

If you can only sample one luxury castle hotel, choose this one. Once the ancestral home of Conor O'Brien, descendant of Brian Ború who defeated the Vikings in 1014, the baronial-style hotel has splendid views over the lake and golf course. Even though the public rooms are awe-inspiringly grand, staff are so friendly that guests quickly feel at home.

Fitzgerald's Woodlands House Hotel

Knockanes, Adare, County Limerick;
tel: 061-605100; www.woodlands-hotel.ie; €€

Price for a double room for one night with breakfast:

€€€€€	over 200 euros
€€€€	160–200 euros
€€€	120–160 euros
€€	90–120 euros
€	under 90 euros

This unpretentious, friendly family-run hotel about a mile outside Adare is a good touring base, within easy reach of Shannon Airport. It has a lively bistro and a more formal restaurant. Constant additions and refurbishment have also given it a pool, a large gym and an above-average spa.

West: the Cliffs of Moher & the Burren

Gregan's Castle

Ballyvaughan, County Clare; tel: 065-707 7005; www.gregans.ie; €€€€€

This is one of Ireland's finest country house hotels, a quiet retreat at the base of the Burren's famous Corkscrew Hill, with breathtaking views over Galway Bay. The elegant decor features fine antiques and contemporary Irish art. A warm welcome and a renowned restaurant make it a favourite hideaway. Be warned, there is only one TV in the house.

Hyland's Burren Hotel

Ballyvaughan, County Clare; tel: 065-707 7037; www.hylandsburren.com; €€; www.burrenwalkinglodge.com; €

Hyland's is a typical, much-extended 19th-century village-centre hotel with a restaurant and lively bar. Most rooms have glorious views of the surrounding limestone hills. The Burren Walking Lodge is under the same management, and offers a simpler but still comfortable alternative.

West: Galway City

The G

Wellpark; tel: 091-865200; www.theghotel.ie; €€€€€

Dedicated followers of fashion will not mind paying a premium to experience a wildly different hotel with an extravagant sense of fun, including a 'vertigo rug' and live seahorses. Designed by hat-maker extrordinaire Philip Treacy, the colourful reception rooms contrast with the soothingly tranquil bedrooms. It also has a seriously good spa. Check out their online offers for 2- or 3-night bargain rates.

The House Hotel

Spanish Parade; tel: 091-538900; www.thehousehotel.ie; €€€

A stylish boutique hotel with a prime location on Galway's 'Left Bank', the House will make a memorable – and convenient – base in the centre of the shopping and pubbing district. Bedrooms in this warehouse conversion are compact but comfortable, with snazzy contemporary decor. The real star here is the House Cocktail Bar (with live music at weekends) and Relax Lounge.

Park House Hotel

Forster Street, Eyre Square; tel: 091-564924; www.parkhousehotel.ie; €€€

An old stone warehouse has been converted and extended to create a welcoming hotel. Bedrooms have warm, colour-coordinated decor and are suf-

Above from far left: striking decor at The G in Galway.

ficiently glazed to mute noisy Galway nights. Right in the city centre, the bar and lobby area are favourites with locals.

West: Connemara

Abbeyglen Castle Hotel

Sky Road, Clifden, County Galway; tel: 095-21201; www.abbeyglen.ie; €€€€

A delightfully old-fashioned manor house hotel, superbly located on a height above Clifden Bay in extensive gardens and only a short walk from town, this is a favourite with Irish holidaymakers, and an ideal base for touring Connemara. The room price includes free afternoon tea, a great rainy day treat. Rooms vary in size and aspect; the best ones are in the front of the house, but all have an old-world charm. At night the bar and restaurant are lively spots.

Ashford Castle

Cong, County Mayo; tel: 094-954 6003; www.ashford.ie; €€€€€

A fairy-tale castle, standing on the isthmus between loughs Corrib and Mask, Ashford never fails to impress.

Price for a double room for one night with breakfast:

€€€€€	over 200 euros
€€€€	160–200 euros
€€€	120–160 euros
€€	90–120 euros
€	under 90 euros

American-owned, it has very high standards of comfort and decor, a private golf course, tennis, fishing, boating, horse riding, falconry, shooting and extensive gardens.

West: Westport Town

Westport Plaza and Castlecourt Hotel

Castlebar Street, Westport town; tel: 098-55088; www.westporthotels resort.ie; €€–€€€

These sister-hotels in the centre of Westport are run by the same family, and share a leisure centre and spa, but have separate identities and facilities. The less expensive Castlecourt is a comfortable, traditional hotel catering for holiday and business clients, while the more snazzy (and more expensive) Plaza is a boutique-style hotel with Chesterfield sofas in its reception area and pleasantly luxurious bedrooms.

Northwest: Sligo Town

Best Western Sligo Southern Hotel

Strandhill Road; tel: 071-916 2101; www.sligosouthernhotel.com; €–€€

A 'superior' 3-star hotel, right in the centre of town (and next to the railway station), with its own leisure centre, bar and broadband access for guests. Although the interior is a little faded, the hotel is excellent value; consider upgrading to a superior room for great views and a private jacuzzi.

Riverside Suites Hotel

Millbrook; tel: 071-914 8080;
www.riversidesuiteshotelsligo.com;
€–€€€

This recent addition to Sligo offers a choice of one- or two-bedroom suites with a riverside setting, complimentary wi-fi and use of the local fitness suite. Book online for large discounts.

Northwest: Donegal Town

Ard na Breatha Guesthouse

Drumrooske Middle; tel: 074-972 2288; www.ardnabreatha.com; €€

An award-winning guesthouse, 2km (1¼ miles) outside Donegal town. The bedrooms are light, bright and spacious, and there is a guest lounge with a small 'honesty bar'. Breakfast choices include the 'full Irish', smoked salmon and pancakes. Highly recommended.

Mill Park

The Mullins; tel: 072-972 2880;
www.millparkhotel.com; €€€

A large hotel close to Donegal town, with a choice of rooms and suites, a leisure centre (including pool, sauna and steam room) and a restaurant specialising in seafood.

Northern Ireland: Belfast

The Merchant Hotel

16 Skipper Street; tel: 028-9023 4888
www.themerchanthotel.com; ££££

The former headquarters of Ulster Bank, an imposing Italianate palazzo, has been exuberantly converted into a luxury hotel while retaining many of the original architectural features. Since opening in 2006 in the arty Cathedral Quarter, this hotel has come to epitomise Belfast's new identity as a hot destination. The huge former banking hall is now the breathtakingly grand Great Room Restaurant.

Tara Lodge

36 Cromwell Road; tel: 028-9059 0900; www.taralodge.com; ££

Well located just off Botanic Avenue, Tara Lodge combines the facilities of a hotel with the friendliness of a guesthouse. The rooms are spacious and comfortable and the staff helpful.

Ten Square Hotel

10 Donegall Square South; tel: 028-9024 1001; www.tensquare.co.uk; ££–£££

A listed Victorian linen warehouse has been transformed into an ultra-luxury hotel with oriental decor and an emphasis on style. Right in the centre of town at Donegall Square.

Price for a double room for one night with breakfast in Northern Ireland:

££££	over £200
£££	£150–200
££	£80–150
£	under £80

Above from far left: pancakes for breakfast; Malmaison Belfast.

After years in the gastronomic wilderness, Ireland has embraced modern cooking with great enthusiasm. Some of the best restaurants in the country are still to be found in hotels, but they are a far cry from the days of overcooked meat and soggy vegetables. Now, a light-handed approach allows the natural flavours of fresh local produce to shine through. Nowhere in Ireland is more than a two-hour drive from the sea, and fresh seafood is a much-prized ingredient. The Irish dining scene is consistently informal: even the grandest hotels specify 'smart but casual', meaning a jacket for men, but no obligatory tie. Advance booking is advisable at weekends and in summer.

While the cities have a wide range of small restaurants, in the countryside pubs are a major element in the eating-out scene. Many are now more like restaurants than the drinking dens of yore, and most welcome children during daylight hours. And thanks to the smoking ban, outdoor tables are commonplace; all you need is the weather to enjoy them.

Dublin

Ananda

2–4 Sandyford Road, Dundrum; tel: 01-296 0099; www.ananda restaurant.ie; daily D, Thur–Sun L; €€€–€€€€

A new restaurant from Atul Kochhar, chef-patron of the Michelin-starred Indian restaurant Benares in London.

The intricate presentation and delicate spicing of the dishes – a wonderful *amuse-bouche* of lentil soup, a divine crab terrine and fabulous thalis – will blow you away. Excellent-value early-bird dinners before 6.30pm.

Chatham Brasserie

Chatham Street; tel: 01-679 0055; www.chathambrasserie.ie; daily 11am–11pm; €€

A modern and stylish all-day brasserie serving European, American and pan-Asian food. Choose from grills, Thai curries or more traditional dishes such as steaks and salmon.

Dunne & Crescenzi

14–16 South Frederick Street; tel: 01-677 3815; www.dunneandcrescenzi.com; Mon–Sat L and D, Sun L only; €–€€

Billed as an authentic *'enoteca Italiana'*, this Italian restaurant and deli is renowned for its simple food and good wine. The prosciutto and mozzarella bars are a particular treat.

Ely Wine Bar

22 Ely Place; tel: 01-676 8986; www.elywinebar.ie; Mon–Fri L and D, Sat D from 5pm; €€–€€€

Just off St Stephen's Green, this Georgian townhouse recalls the gracious Dublin of old. The list of over 400 wines, many by the glass, is renowned. Traditional fare, including rare breed

pork sausages, steaks of organic and dry-aged beef, is largely sourced on the family farm in County Clare, while seafood is fresh from the Atlantic. A much bigger and contemporary Ely gastropub and a brasserie *(see website)* are in the same family.

Market Bar

Fade Street; tell 01-613 9094; www. marketbar.ie; food served Mon–Thur noon–11.30pm, Fri–Sat noon–1.30am, Sun noon–11pm; €€

A gorgeous cavernous bar serving an exciting selection of tapas – Cajun sea trout, steamed mussels, beef stew – in small or large portions, with a good choice of wine.

Yamamori Noodles

71–72 South Great George's Street (sushi bar: on 38–39 Lower Ormond Quay); tel: 01-475 5001; www.yamam orinoodles.ie; Sun–Wed noon–10.30pm, Thur–Sat until 11.30pm; €–€€

A popular Japanese restaurant serving freshly prepared noodles, sushi and ramen. Try the clay seafood hotpot or the good-value daily bento-box specials.

Price guide for a two-course dinner for one:	
€€€€	over 40 euros
€€€	30–40 euros
€€	20–30 euros
€	under 20 euros

Around Dublin: County Wicklow

Roundwood Inn

Roundwood (N11); tel: 01-281 8107; bar menu daily noon–9.30pm, restaurant Fri–Sat D, Sun L; €€–€€€

Situated in Wicklow's highest village, en route to Glendalough, this 17th-century inn serves Irish-German fusion cuisine, with an emphasis on locally sourced meat and fish for dishes such as crab bisque, Wicklow trout, suckling pig and, in winter, roasted stuffed goose.

Southeast: County Wexford

Harvest Room Restaurant

Dunbrody Country House Hotel, Arthurstown, New Ross; tel: 051-389600; www.dunbrodyhouse.com; Mon–Sun D, Sun L; €€€€

Talented TV chef Kevin Dundon serves some of Irish cuisine's most spectacular food at this small luxury hotel. The emphasis is on simple but imaginative combinations of fresh ingredients. The elaborate desserts are legendary. There is also a more informal Champagne & Seafood Bar (daily 2–10pm, Sun from 3.30pm; €€) with a choice of 16 items in starter-size portions.

Southeast: County Waterford

The Tannery

10 Quay Street, Dungarvan; tel: 058-45420; www.tannery.ie; Tue–Fri L and D, Sat D, Sun L; €€–€€€

An old stone warehouse has been con-

Above from far left: Hugo's bar and restaurant in Dublin *(see p.39)*.

verted into a minimalist first-floor restaurant. Owner-chef Paul Flynn's cooking attracts food lovers from miles away. Simple menus based on local ingredients are inspired by Mediterranean and global cuisine. Start with crab crème brûlée with pickled cucumber, followed by slow-cooked ox cheek.

Southwest: Cork City

Café Paradiso

16 Lancaster Quay, Western Road; tel: 021-427 7939; www.cafeparadiso. ie; Tue–Thur D, Fri–Sat L and D; €–€€€

Owner-cook Denis Cotter has transformed the reputation of vegetarian cooking at his small but stylish restaurant. Even carnivores look forward to his imaginative, robustly spiced combinations of seasonal fare: in summer, perhaps, eggroll pancake of asparagus and Coolea cheese with a warm cherry tomato and fennel salsa, in autumn the signature pumpkin risotto.

Greenes

48 MacCurtain Street; 021-455 2279; Mon–Sat B and D; €€

Turn off busy MacCurtain Street into

Price guide for a two-course dinner for one:

€€€€	over 40 euros
€€€	30–40 euros
€€	20–30 euros
€	under 20 euros

a small cobblestoned alley for a pleasant surprise: at night this Victorian warehouse conversion is floodlit and a natural waterfall runs down one wall, by day there are outdoor tables. Seafood is the speciality here, but meat and vegetarian food is also offered in Mediterranean-style dishes and Asian-influenced fusion cuisine.

Southwest: West Cork Coast

Fishy Fishy Restaurant

Crowley's Pier, Kinsale; tel: 021-470 0415; www.fishyfishy.ie; daily L and D; €€–€€€

One of Ireland's leading seafood restaurants occupies two floors of a substantial house in the town park. If you have never tried real scampi made from freshly caught prawns, do so here. The salads are huge, with the warm seafood salad a lunchtime favourite.

Mary Ann's

Castletownshend, Skibbereen; tel: 028-36146; www.maryannsbarrest aurant.com; daily L and D, Oct–Apr Tue–Sat only; bar €, restaurant €€€

Said to be one of the oldest bars in Ireland, this dream gastropub is hidden away in a picturesque fishing village. Packed in summer, with a large patio, it's even more charming in winter, when there might be only a few diners in the low-ceilinged bar. Daily specials include hot crab gratin or lobster thermidor, while the seafood platter is legendary.

Southwest: Dingle Town

The Chart House

The Mall, Dingle; tel: 066-915 2255;
www.thecharthousedingle.com;
June–Sept daily D, Oct–May phone
to confirm; €€

The bright red half-door of Jim Mc-Carthy's stone-built cottage restaurant is the first thing you see on arriving at Dingle. A favourite starter is local black pudding in filo pastry with apple and date chutney and hollandaise sauce. Pork is served with brandied apples, pan-fried brill with smoked bacon and rocket. Desserts are a highlight.

West: Limerick City & Shannon

Brasserie One

1 Pery Square, Limerick; tel: 061-402 402; www.oneperysquare.com;
€–€€€

This hotel in a tall Georgian town house is close to the city centre overlooking the People's Park. Bar food is served in a pleasant lounge on the ground floor, while the elegant but informal brasserie is on the first floor. Food from the Franco-Irish menu is freshly prepared to order.

The Wild Geese

Rose Cottage, Main Street, Adare;
tel: 061-396451; www.thewild-geese.
com; Tue–Sat D, Sun L; €€€

Located in one of Adare's thatched cottages, this is a serious restaurant, with a well-travelled owner-chef offering excellent modern Irish cuisine. The menu is luxurious, with wide choice. Seared scallops and chorizo are are served on buttered leeks, while marinated loin of venison comes with savoy cabbage and parsnip purée.

West: the Cliffs of Moher & the Burren

Moran's Oyster Cottage

Kilcolgan; tel: 091-796113;
www.moransoystercottage.com;
daily L and D; €–€€

One of the quintessential west of Ireland experiences is a seafood feast at Moran's. The tiny thatched pub is 500m/yds off the N18 (signposted in Kilcolgan), beside a wide weir and the Moran family's oyster beds. The front bar has been preserved, but there is also a large restaurant behind. Local oysters are in season from September to April, in summer there's crab and lobster.

West: Galway City

Kirwan's Lane Restaurant

Kirwan's Lane; tel: 091-568266;
Mon–Sat L and D; €€–€€€

Kirwan's Lane is a quiet medieval alleyway off Galway's long main street, and the restaurant is a smart, contemporary space on two airy levels. The cuisine is contemporary Irish, with some unusual combinations: smoked haddock and clam chowder with lime crème fraîche, while saddle of rabbit is served with black pudding stuffing.

Viña Mara

19 Middle Street; tel: 091-561610;
www.avinamara.com; Tue–Sat L; €
and D; €€

This former shop is now an intimate
restaurant serving food, sourced locally
when possible. Among the chef's specialities is potted salmon with seaweed
butter, and slow-cooked Irish beef.

West: Connemara

Leenane Hotel

Leenane, Co Mayo; tel: 095-42249;
www.leenanehotel.com; L and D
daily, Easter to mid-Nov; €

This venerable old hotel overlooking
Killary Fjord serves bar food beside the
open fire in the bar at lunchtime. In the
evening the dining room is packed with
savvy punters tucking into a great value
menu. This includes baked Killary Bay
salmon with lime beurre blanc, and
rack of Connemara mountain lamb.

Owenmore Restaurant

Ballynahinch Hotel, Recess; tel:
095-31006; www.ballynahinch-
castle.com; bar daily L and D; €€;
restaurant daily D; €€€€.

It's not really a castle but a massive
Victorian mansion with crenellations,
set in romantic woodland on the Ballynahinch River. The five-course set
dinner menu offers a wide choice of
classic dishes, including local game.
Meals are also served in the bar.

West: Westport Town

La Fougère

Knockranny House Hotel and Spa;
tel: 098-28600; www.khh.ie; daily L
€€ and D; €€€€

This Victorian-style hotel was built
on an elevated site overlooking the
town. The hotel dining room, La
Fougère (The Fern) has views across
the town to Croaghpatrick and Clew
Bay, and creates a sense of occasion
with its traditional table settings. The
menus offer a wide choice of fine local
produce, including Mayo mountain
lamb and Clare Island salmon.

Northwest: Sligo Town

Hargadon's Bar

4–5 O'Connell Street; tel: 071-915
3709; www.hargadons.com;
Mon–Sat L and D; €

One of Ireland's great traditional
pubs, its interior has changed very
little since its opening back in 1864.
The restaurant serves a simple menu
of hearty fare, much of it organic
and locally produced – from oysters
to crab linguini to bangers and mash
or farmhouse cheese platter – at
great prices.

Price guide for a two-
course dinner for one in
the Republic:

€€€€	over 40 euros
€€€	30–40 euros
€€	20–30 euros
€	under 20 euros

Olde Castle Bar and Red Hugh's Restaurant

Tirconnell Street; tel: 074-972 1262;
www.oldecastlebar.com; L Mon–Sat,
€; D daily June–Sept; Thur–Sun,
Sat–Sun off season; €€

An old stone-built bar across the street from the town's famous castle serves great bar food at lunch, including Irish Stew (lamb and root vegetables in broth). At night the upstairs restaurant has a great reputation for local seafood, from battered haddock to oysters and lobster.

La Boca

6 Fountain Street; tel: 028-9032
3087; www.labocabelfast.com;
Mon–Wed 9am–10pm, Thur–Sat
9am–10pm, Fri–Sat 10.30am–10pm;
££

La Boca is a buzzing little place with live music, big steaks and great service. The all-day bistro menu of Argentine and Spanish specials is supplemented by an afternoon *picadas* (small plates) menu, which offers figs, manchego cheese, olives and cured meats.

Cayenne

Shaftesbury Square; tel: 028-9033
1532; www.cayenne-restaurant.co.uk;
Thur–Fri L, daily D; ££

Run by celebrity chef Paul Rankin, this funky restaurant's avant-garde interior is always buzzing. It is worth seeking out for its pan-Asian cooking, served alongside Irish favourites such as chargrilled sirloin with ox tongue and cheek, and inspired desserts.

Metro Brasserie

13 Lower Crescent; tel: 028-9032
3349; www.crescenttownhouse.com;
daily D; ££–£££

This elegant brasserie just off Botanic Avenue offers modern Irish and British cooking with a twist; try the slow-roast pork belly, fish of the day or breast of Gressingham duck with celeriac dauphinois. There's also a comprehensive vegetarian menu and an excellent choice of wines.

Mourne Seafood Bar

34–36 Bank Street; tel: 028-9024
8544; www.mourneseafood.com;
Mon noon–6pm, Tue–Sat
noon–9.30pm, Sun 1–6pm; £–££

One of the city's favourite restaurants, this seafood bar serves up the daily catch from the owners' beds in Calingford Lough, and the ports of Annalong and Kilkeel. The Mourne seafood casserole is renowned.

Above from far left: Belfast has a top-class restaurant scene; Cayenne.

Price guide for a two-course dinner for one in Northern Ireland	
££££	over £40
£££	£25–40
££	£15–25
£	under £15

Aside from Irish dancing and Irish pubs, Ireland offers state-of-the-art theatres and auditoria. Some of the main venues are listed here.

The two capitals and Cork, Galway, Limerick and Sligo all have thriving live music scenes; check the local papers for details (and for Dublin and Belfast, *see also margin, right*).

Dublin

Abbey Theatre
Lower Abbey Street; tel: 01-878 7222; www.abbeytheatre.ie
Founded in 1903 by W.B. Yeats and Lady Gregory, the Abbey rejuvenated Irish literature and culture. Ireland's national theatre still features many Irish classics in its programme. The Abbey's sister theatre, the Peacock, stages new work.

Gaiety Theatre
South King Street; tel: 01-677 1717; www.gaietytheatre.ie
A fine Victorian building, recently restored, with a programme that includes opera, ballet, pantomime, variety concerts and serious drama.

Gate Theatre
1 Cavendish Row, Parnell Square; tel: 01-874 4045; www.gate-theatre.ie
Founded in 1928, the Gate stages avant-garde European, Irish and American theatre by playwrights such as Samuel Beckett, Brian Friel and Arthur Miller.

Olympia Theatre
72 Dame Street; tel: 01-679 3323; www.olympia.ie
One of the oldest theatres in Dublin, the Olympia was once a Victorian music hall; now it is used both as a theatre and as a venue for live bands.

Project Arts Centre
39 East Essex Street, Temple Bar; tel: 01-881 9613; www.projectarts centre.ie
This arts centre stages cutting-edge music and performance shows, as well as contemporary art exhibitions.

Samuel Beckett Theatre
Trinity College; tel: 01-896 1334; www.tcd.ie/drama
The Beckett is based in the university that produced such dramatists as Goldsmith, Synge and Beckett himself, and is run in association with the university's Samuel Beckett Centre. It's a venue for both the Dublin Fringe and Dublin Theatre festivals.

Southwest: Cork City

Everyman Palace
15 MacCurtain Street; tel: 021-450 1673; www.everymanpalace.com
This 650-seat late-Victorian theatre stages drama and musicals, and also hosts club nights.

Cork Opera House
Emmet Place; tel: 021-427 0022; www.corkoperahouse.ie

Cork's principal theatre since the late 19th century offers drama, musicals, family shows, dance and comedy.

Siamsa Tíre: National Folk Theatre of Ireland

Town Park, Tralee; tel: 066-712 3055; www.siamsatire.com
The Irish rural tradition is celebrated here in song, dance and mime.

Belltable Arts Centre

36 Cecil Street; tel: 061-319 866; www.belltable.ie
A venue for film, comedy, drama, visual arts and improvisational acts.

Glór Irish Music Centre

Causeway Link; tel: 065-684 3103; www.glor.ie
A modern building with two auditoria. Irish music shows in summer; theatre and comedy for the rest of the year.

Druid Theatre Company

Druid Lane Theatre, Druid Lane; tel: 091-568 660; www.druidtheatre.com
One of Ireland's most successful repertory theatre companies presents a mix of new work and revivals in its recently refurbished 90-seat theatre. Other companies perform at the Town Hall Theatre (Courthouse Square; 091-569777; www.tht.ie).

Hawk's Well Theatre

Temple Street; tel: 071-916 1518; www.hawkswell.com
A modern theatre that hosts touring and local shows; home of the annual W.B. Yeats International Summer School.

Grand Opera House

Great Victoria Street; tel: 028-9024 1919; www.goh.co.uk
This glorious 1895 building is Belfast's biggest entertainment venue, staging drama, musicals, ballet and pantomime.

Lyric Theatre

Ridgeway Street; tel: 028-9038 1081; www.lyrictheatre.co.uk
Northern Ireland's only full-time producing theatre has an £18m state-of-the-art building on the banks of the River Lagan with a bar and café.

The MAC

Hurst House, 18–19 Corporation Square; tel: 028-9023 5053; www.themaclive.com
A multi-discipline arts centre in Belfast's Cathedral Quarter with two theatres and three art galleries.

Waterfront Hall

2 Lanyon Place; tel: 028-9033 4455; www.waterfront.co.uk
A multi-purpose venue offering comedy, theatre, music and acrobatics, with two exhibition galleries.

Above from far left: Dublin's drinking Mecca; live music in Belfast.

Where's the Craic?
The Irish will gladly pursue the *craic* for several hours until they find it. If you are looking for live music, ask around, particularly in smaller towns; a local barperson will usually know which bar or venue has live sounds that evening. Impromptu music sessions, or even recitations of stories or poetry, are common.

In Dublin the Temple Bar Music Centre (Curved Street; www.tbmc.ie) hosts hip-hop, jazz and classical; for rock, pop and folk, try Village (26 Wexford Street; www.the villagevenue.com) or Whelans (25 Wexford Street; www. whelanslive.com). In Belfast try The John Hewitt (51 Donegall Street; www.thejohn hewitt.com) for blues, jazz and folk, or Madden's Bar (74 Berry Street) for traditional Irish music.

CREDITS

Insight Step by Step Ireland
Written by: Alannah Hopkin and Tara Stubbs
Updated by: Alannah Hopkin
Commissioning Editor: Sarah Sweeney
Series Editor: Carine Tracanelli
Map Production: APA Cartography Department and Stephen Ramsay
Picture Manager: Yoshimi Kanazawa
Art Editor: Richard Cooke
Production: Tynan Dean and Linton Donaldson

Principal Photographer: Corrie Wingate
Photography by: All pictures © APA/Corrie Wingate and APA Glyn Genin except: Bantry House 58B; Corbis 25T; Fáilte Ireland 44/45, 46TL/TR, 47TL; Granville Hotel 110T, 112T, 113T; iStockphoto: 7C, 17TL, 26TL, 45TR, 48T, 54T, 56TR, 65TR, 66/67, 90TL, 91B/T, 93TR, 95; Leonardo 108T, 109T; Malmaison 115T; Northern Ireland Tourist Board 20B, 92/93, 92TL, 94T, 95T, 112T, 124/125; Tourism Ireland 44B/T, 47TR, 60/61.
Front cover: main image: 4Corners Images; bottom images: Ireland Tourist Board.
Acknowledgements: Tara would like to thank Lucy Wyatt for all her help.

Printed by: CTPS-China

Although Insight Guides and the authors of this book have taken all reasonable care in preparing it, we make no warranty about the accuracy or completeness of its content, and, to the maximum extent permitted, disclaim all liability arising from its use.

CONTACTING THE EDITORS

We would appreciate it if readers would alert us to errors or outdated information by writing to us at insight@apaguide.co.uk or APA Publications, PO Box 7910, London SE1 1WE, UK.

www.insightguides.com

DISTRIBUTION

Worldwide
APA Publications GmbH & Co. Verlag KG
(Singapore branch)
7030 Ang Mo Kio Ave 5
08-65 Northstar @ AMK, Singapore 569880
Email: apasin@singnet.com.sg

UK and Ireland
Dorling Kindersley Ltd,
(a Penguin Company)
80 Strand, London, WC2R 0RL, UK
Email: customerservice@uk.dk.com

US
Ingram Publisher Services
One Ingram Blvd, PO Box 3006
La Vergne, TN 37086-1986
Email: customer.service@ingrampublisher
services.com

Australia
Universal Publishers
PO Box 307
St. Leonards, NSW 1590
Email: sales@universalpublishers.com.au

New Zealand
Brown Knows Publications
11 Artesia Close, Shamrock Park
Auckland, New Zealand 2016
Email: sales@brownknows.co.nz

INDEX

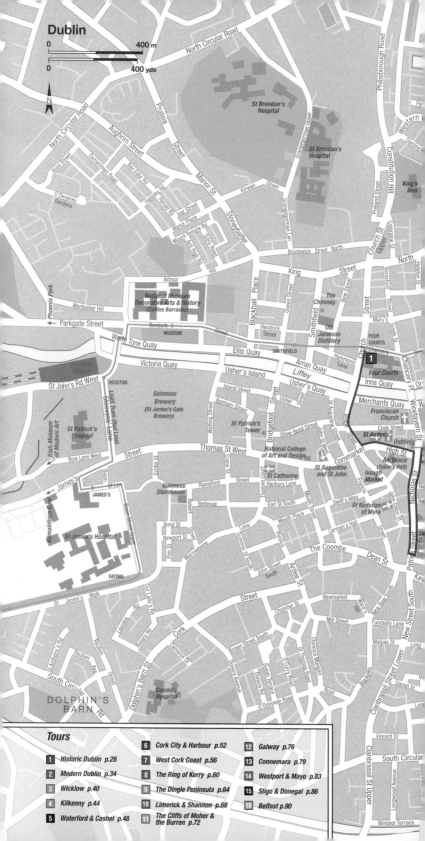

Dublin

0 ────────── 400 m
0 ────────── 400 yds

N

North Circular Road

Phibsborough Road

St Brendan's Hospital

St Brendan's Hospital

King's Inns

North Circular Road

Ross Street

O'Devaney Gardens

Aughrim Street

Oxmantown Road

Ben Edar Rd

Halliday Rd

Manor Place

Arbour Hill

Mount Temple Rd

Stirrup Road

Prussia Street

Manor St

Kirwan Street

Stoneybatter

Brunswick Street North

King Street

Blackhall Place

Queen Street

Smithfield

The Chimney

Bow Street

Church St Upper

North

Arbour Hill

National Museum Decorative Arts & History (Collins Barracks)

Benburb Street

MUSEUM

Hendrick Street

Old Jameson Distillery

Mary's

FOUR COURTS

Chancery

Montpelier Hill

Parkgate Street

Phoenix Park

Wolfe Tone Quay

Victoria Quay

Ellis Quay

SMITHFIELD

Arran Quay

Liffey

Hammond Lane

Four Courts

Four Courts

Chancery Pl

Heuston Station

St John's Rd West

HEUSTON

LUAS Tram (Red Line) STEEVENS' LANE

Guinness Brewery (St James's Gate Brewery)

Usher's Island

Island Street

Bonham Street

St Augustine St

Usher

Usher's Quay

Inns Quay

Merchants Quay

Franciscan Church

St Audoen

Dublinia

St Patrick's Hospital

Irish Museum of Modern Art

Bow Lane West

Street

Eoghin St

Crane St

Thomas St West

Watling Street

Bridgefoot Street

St Patrick's Tower

Oliver Bond St

John St West

National College of Art and Design

St Augustine and St John

Commarket

High St

An Taisce (Tailor's Hall) Iveagh Market

Cook Street

St James's Hospital

JAMES'S

St Lsn

Guinness Storehouse

Rainsford Street

Robert

Thomas Court

St Catherine

Hanbury Lane

Bellevue

Earl St South

Meath Street

Swift's Alley

St Nicholas of Myra

John Dillon St

Nicholas St

Patrick Street

Kilmainham La

JAMES'S

Basin St Lwr

Bond St

Newport St

Pim St

Marrowbone

Summer St South

Meath Place

Carman's Hall

FATIMA

St James's Walk

Our Lady's Rd

Rosary Rd

Reuben Street

The Coombe

John Street South

Ardee St

Dean St

Newmarket

Ward's Hill

New Row South

Key

South Circular

St Anthony's Rd

Reuben Ave

South Circular Road

Cork Street

Cameron St

Brown Street South

Mill Street

Fumbally Lane

Malpas St

Clanbrassil Street Lower

DOLPHIN'S BARN

Dolphin's Barn Rd

Chamber St

Coombe Hospital

Sylvan Terrace

St Thomas Road

Donore Avenue

O'Donovan Road

Road

Blackpitts

New Street South

Daniel St

Vincent St

Clanbrassil St Upper

South Circular

Longwood Avenue

Windsor Terrace

Tours